Michael Price

Excel
2019

in
easy steps

In easy steps is an imprint of In Easy Steps Limited
16 Hamilton Terrace · Holly Walk · Leamington Spa
Warwickshire · United Kingdom · CV32 4LY
www.ineasysteps.com

Notice of Liability
Every effort has been made to ensure that this book contains accurate
and current information. However, In Easy Steps Limited and the
author shall not be liable for any loss or damage suffered by readers
as a result of any information contained herein.

Trademarks
Microsoft® and Windows® are registered trademarks of Microsoft
Corporation. All other trademarks are acknowledged as belonging to
their respective companies.

In Easy Steps Limited supports The Forest Stewardship Council (FSC),
the leading international forest certification organization. All our titles
that are printed on Greenpeace approved FSC certified paper carry the
FSC logo.

MIX
Paper from
responsible sources
FSC® C020837

Printed and bound in the United Kingdom

ISBN 978-1-84078-821-1

Contents

1 Introduction   7

The Spreadsheet Concept	8
Microsoft Excel	10
Microsoft Office 2019	11
System Requirements	12
Getting Office 2019	13
Excel 2019 and Windows 10	14
The Office 2019 Ribbon	16
Exploring Excel 2019	18
Excel Online App	20

2 Begin with Excel   21

The Excel Window	22
Create a Workbook	24
Add Data to the Worksheet	25
Build the Worksheet	26
Fill Cells	28
Complete the Worksheet	29
Format the Text	30
Format the Numbers	31
Print the Worksheet	32
Insert, Copy and Paste	34
Excel Help	35
Contextual Help	36
Excel File Formats	37

3 Manage Data   39

Use Existing Data	40
Import Data	42
Navigate the Worksheet	44
Scroll with the Wheel Mouse	46
Keystrokes and Touch	47
Sort Rows	48
Find Entries	49
Filter Information	50
Remove Duplicate Entries	52
Check Spelling	53
Freeze Headers and Labels	54
Hide Columns or Rows	55
Protect a Worksheet	56

4 Formulas and Functions — 57

Number Formats — 58
Text Formats — 60
Relative References — 61
Absolute References — 62
Name References — 63
Operators — 64
Calculation Sequence — 65
Functions — 66
AutoSum — 68
Formula Errors — 69
Add Comments — 70

5 Excel Tables — 71

Create an Excel Table — 72
Edit Tables — 74
Table Styles — 75
Table Totals — 76
Count Unique Entries — 77
Structured References — 78
Calculated Columns — 79
Insert Rows — 80
Custom Sort — 82
Print a Table — 83
Summarize a Table — 84
Convert to a Range — 86

6 Advanced Functions — 87

Function Library — 88
Logical Functions — 89
Lookup/Reference Functions — 90
Financial Functions — 92
Date & Time Functions — 94
Text Functions — 96
Math & Trig Functions — 98
Random Numbers — 100
Statistical Functions — 101
Engineering Functions — 102
Excel Add-ins — 103
Evaluate Formula — 104

7   Control Excel   105

Audit Formulas	106
Protect Formulas	108
Check for Errors	109
Backup	111
AutoSave and AutoRecover	112
Startup Switches	113
Create a Shortcut	114
Ribbon Key Tips	115
Using Key Tips	116
Collapse the Ribbon	118
Quick Access Toolbar	119
Mini Toolbar	120
Print Worksheets	121

8   Charts   123

Create a Chart	124
Recommended Chart Type	126
Change Chart Layout	127
Legend and Data Table	128
Change Chart Type	129
Pie Chart	130
3-D Pie Chart	132
3-D Column Chart	133
Share Price Data	134
Line Chart	135
Stock Chart	136
Mixed Types	137
Print Charts	138

9   Macros in Excel   139

Macros	140
Create Macros	141
Record a Macro	142
Apply the Macro	144
View the Macro	145
Macro to Make a Table	146
Edit the Macro	148
Use the Macro	149
Create Macros with VBA	150
Add Macros to the Toolbar	152
Debug Macros	154

10 Templates and Scenarios   155

Templates   156
Online Templates   158
More Excel Resources   160
What-If Analysis   162
Summary Reports   164
Goal Seek   166
Optimization   167
Project Worksheet   168
Solver   169

11 Links and Connections   171

Link to Workbooks   172
Create External References   174
Styles of Reference   176
Source Workbook Changes   177
Apply the Updates   178
Turn Off the Prompt   179
Save Workbook Online   180
Using the Excel Online App   182
Excel in Word   184
Publish as PDF (or XPS)   186

Index   187

1 Introduction

This chapter shows how the spreadsheet, the electronic counterpart of the paper ledger, has evolved in Excel, taking advantage of the various features of Microsoft Office, and the Windows operating system.

8 The Spreadsheet Concept

10 Microsoft Excel

11 Microsoft Office 2019

12 System Requirements

13 Getting Office 2019

14 Excel 2019 and Windows 10

16 The Office 2019 Ribbon

18 Exploring Excel 2019

20 Excel Online App

The Spreadsheet Concept

Spreadsheets, in the guise of the accountant's ledger sheet, have been in use for many, many years. They consisted of paper forms with a two-dimensional grid of rows and columns, often on extra-large paper, forming two pages of a ledger book, for example (hence the term "spread sheet"). They were typically used by accountants to prepare budget or financial statements. Each row would represent a different item, with each column showing the value or amount for that item over a given time period. For example, a forecast for a 30% margin (mark-up) and 10% growth might show:

Ledger sheets pre-date computers and handheld calculators, and have been in use for literally hundreds of years.

				Profit Forecast		
Margin %	30					
Growth %	10					
		January	February	March	April	May
Cost of Goods		6,000	6,600	7,260	7,986	8,785
Sales		7,800	8,580	9,438	10,382	11,420
Profit		1,800	1,980	2,178	2,396	2,635
Total Profit		1,800	3,780	5,958	8,354	10,989

Any changes to the basic figures would mean that all the values would have to be recalculated and transcribed to another ledger sheet to show the effect; e.g. for a 20% margin and 60% growth:

				Profit Forecast		
Margin %	20					
Growth %	60					
		January	February	March	April	May
Cost of Goods		6,000	9,600	15,360	24,576	39,322
Sales		7,200	11,520	18,432	29,491	47,186
Profit		1,200	1,920	3,072	4,915	7,864
Total Profit		1,200	3,120	6,192	11,107	18,972

The first spreadsheet application was VisiCorp's VisiCalc (visible calculator). Numerous competitive programs appeared, but market leadership was taken first by Lotus 123, and now by Microsoft Excel.

To make another change – to show 10% margin and 200% growth, for example – would involve a completely new set of calculations. And, each time, there would be the possibility of a calculation or transcription error creeping in.

With the advent of the personal computer, a new approach became possible. Applications were developed to simulate the operation of the financial ledger sheet, but the boxes (known as cells) that formed the rows and columns could store text, numbers, or a calculation formula based on the contents of other cells. The spreadsheet looked the same, since it was the results that were displayed, rather than the formulas themselves. However, when the contents of a cell were changed in the spreadsheet, all the cells whose values depended on that changed cell would be automatically recalculated.

This new approach allowed a vast improvement in productivity for various activities, such as forecasting. In the second example shown on the previous page, you'd set up the initial spreadsheet using formulas, rather than calculating the individual cell values. A spreadsheet might contain these values and formulas, for example:

	A	B	C	D	E
1	Margin%	30			
2	Growth%	10			
3					Profit Forecast
4			Jan	Feb	Mar
5	Cost of Goods		6000	=C5+C5*$B$2/100	=D5+D5*$B$2/100
6	Sales		=C5*(100+$B$1)/100	=D5*(100+$B$1)/100	=E5*(100+$B$1)/100
7	Profit		=C6-C5	=D6-D5	=E6-E5
8	Total Profit		=C7	=C8+D7	=D8+E7
9					

However, what will be displayed in the cells are the actual values that the formulas compute, based on the contents of the cells that the formulas refer to:

	A	B	C	D	E	F	G	H
1	Margin%	30						
2	Growth%	10						
3					Profit Forecast			
4			Jan	Feb	Mar	Apr	May	
5	Cost of Goods		6000	6600	7260	7986	8785	
6	Sales		7800	8580	9438	10382	11420	
7	Profit		1800	1980	2178	2396	2635	
8	Total Profit		1800	3780	5958	8354	10989	
9								

When you want to see the effect of changes – such as different values for margin and growth, for example – you change just those items and instantly see the effect, as the values calculated by the formulas are adjusted and redisplayed. The capabilities of the spreadsheet applications have evolved, and the use of spreadsheets has extended far beyond the original use for financial planning and reporting. They can now handle any activity that involves arrays of values interrelated by formulas; grading examination scores; interpreting experimental data; or keeping track of assets and inventories, for example. In fact, the newest spreadsheet applications seem to support just about any possible requirement that can be imagined.

Microsoft Excel

VisiCalc and Lotus 123 were MS-DOS programs, subject to its command-line interface, but Microsoft Excel was developed for Windows. It was the first spreadsheet program to allow users to control the visual aspects of the spreadsheet (fonts, character attributes, and cell appearance). It introduced intelligent cell recomputation, where only cells dependent on the cell being modified are updated (previous spreadsheet programs recomputed everything all the time, or waited for a specific Recalc command). Later versions of Excel were shipped as part of the bundled Microsoft Office suite of applications, which included programs like Microsoft Word and Microsoft PowerPoint. Versions of Excel for Microsoft Windows and Office include:

There are also versions of Excel designed specifically for the Apple Macintosh ("Mac") computers – starting from Excel 1.0! Excel 2019 is available in versions for mobile devices that use iOS, such as the iPad and the iPhone. There are also versions for cell phones and tablets that are Android- or Windows-based.

1987	Excel 2.0	Windows
1990	Excel 3.0	Windows
1992	Excel 4.0	Windows
1993	Excel 5.0	Windows
1995	Excel 95 (v7.0)	Office 95
1997	Excel 97 (v8.0)	Office 97
1999	Excel 2000 (v9.0)	Office 2000
2001	Excel 2002 (v10)	Office XP
2003	Excel 2003 (v11)	Office 2003
2007	Excel 2007 (v12)	Office 2007
2010	Excel 2010 (v14)	Office 2010
2013	Excel 2013 (v15)	Office 2013 / Office 365
2015	Excel 2016 (v16)	Office 2016 / Office 365
2018	Excel 2019 (v18)	Office 2019 / Office 365

The newer versions of Excel provide many enhancements to the user interface, and incorporate connections with Microsoft Office and other applications. The basis of the program, however, remains the same. It still consists of a large array of cells, organized into rows and columns, containing data values or formulas with relative or absolute references to other cells. This means that many of the techniques included in this book will be applicable to whichever version of Excel you may be using, or even if you are using a spreadsheet from another family of products; though, of course, the specifics of the instructions may need to be adjusted.

The New icon pictured above indicates new or enhanced features introduced in Excel 2019.

Microsoft Office 2019

Microsoft Office 2019 is the latest version of Microsoft Office, and it is available in a variety of editions, including:

- **Office Home & Student 2019 (PC & Mac)**
- **Office Home & Business 2019 (PC & Mac)**
- **Office Professional 2019**

There are volume licensing versions for larger organizations:

- **Office Standard 2019 (PC & Mac)**
- **Office Professional Plus 2019**

There is also a subscription version of Microsoft Office known as Office 365, and this is also available in a number of editions:

- **Office 365 Home (PC & Mac)**
- **Office 365 Personal (PC & Mac)**
- **Office 365 University**
- **Office 365 Business**
- **Office 365 Enterprise**

All of these editions include Microsoft Excel 2019. Whichever edition you obtain, your copy of Excel 2019 incorporates all the features and uses the Office result-oriented user interface, with the Ribbon, File tab, BackStage, Galleries, and Live Preview; etc.

Excel 2019 also uses the Microsoft Office file format, OpenXML, as the default file format. This is based on XML and uses ZIP compression, so the files will be up to 75% smaller than those in the older Microsoft Office file formats.

Other shared Office features include the Document Theme, which defines colors, fonts, and graphic effects for a spreadsheet or other Office document, and collaboration services for sharing spreadsheets and documents with other users.

The Office Online apps work in conjunction with OneDrive, the online storage associated with your Microsoft Account (or your Office 365 Account, if you have a subscription).

Office Online

Microsoft offers a free, web-based version of Office; this includes online versions of Word, Excel, PowerPoint, and OneNote. These online products feature user interfaces similar to the full desktop products, and allow you to access Office documents, including Excel spreadsheets, via your browser. They also make it easier for you to share documents with users who may not have Office 2019 on their systems. However, the Office Online apps do not support the full feature set of the desktop products.

System Requirements

To install and run Excel 2019, your computer should match or better the minimum hardware and operating system requirements for Office 2019. If you are upgrading to Office 2019, from Office 2010 or Office 2013, the hardware should already meet the requirements – though you may need to upgrade your operating system. For an upgrade from earlier versions of Office you will need to check that both hardware and operating system meet the minimum specifications for Office 2019. This includes:

Operating system	Windows 10 (32-bit or 64-bit) or Windows Server 2019 (64-bit)
Processor	1.6 GHz or higher (32-bit or 64-bit)
Memory	2 GB (32-bit) or 4 GB (64-bit)
Hard disk	4 GB of available disk space
Monitor	1280 x 768 resolution or higher
Internet	Broadband connection recommended for download, product activation and OneDrive

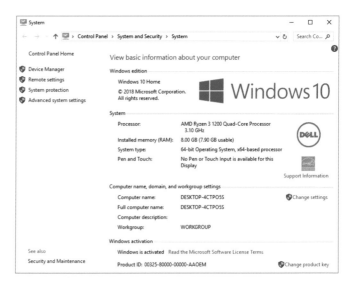

Microsoft Office Compatibility Pack

This allows a computer running an older version of Office (2000, XP or 2003) to work with documents in the format used by later versions, including Office 2019. Microsoft no longer provides this software, but you can download a copy from **www.softpedia.com** This will allow older versions of Excel to read the new file format.

These are minimum requirements. You may need other components (e.g. a sound card) for some Excel features.

Office 2019 (32-bit) runs on both 32-bit and 64-bit systems. Microsoft recommends this, rather than the 64-bit version, for add-in compatibility.

This software only runs under Windows 2003, Vista, XP and 2000, and it only works with Office 2000, XP and 2003. If possible, save your Office 2019 documents in Office 97-2003 format for the older systems.

Getting Office 2019

You can buy your preferred version of Microsoft Office 2019 in disk format from a retail source, or download it from Microsoft. Windows 10 provides the "Get Office" app, which checks the status of Office on your machine and, if it isn't currently installed, helps you to obtain a copy.

 Click the **Get Office** Start Menu tile or All Apps entry to review the status of Office on your system

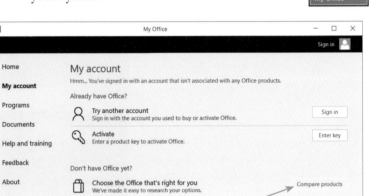

If you have been given a product key for Office, select Enter key and follow the prompts to download your copy.

 Choose **Compare products** to view the options that are available; for example, Office 365 Home (Subscription) or Office Home & Student 2019 (One-time purchase)

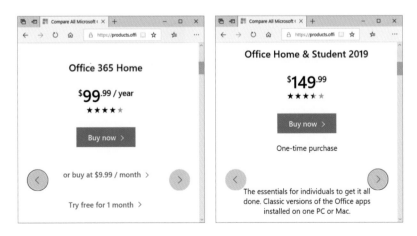

Microsoft is keen to encourage adoption of the subscription versions – Office 365 Personal edition offers a free trial and also includes 60 minutes per month of Skype calls to cell phones and landlines.

 Choose your preference and follow the prompts to buy and download the selected version

Excel 2019 and Windows 10

With Microsoft Office 2019 installed under Windows 10, you have a number of ways to launch Excel 2019:

1 Your installation of Office may have added icons for Office applications on the Windows Desktop Taskbar. Click the green **X** icon to launch Excel 2019

Right-click Excel on the **All apps** list and select **Pin to Start** to add the Excel tile.

2 Alternatively, you may find tiles for the Office applications on the Start screen. Click the Excel tile

3 If icons or tiles aren't shown, select **Start** and scroll the **All Apps** list to the **E** category and click the **Excel** entry

Right-click Excel on the **All apps** list, click **More** and click **Pin to taskbar** to add the Excel icon.

You can also look for applications by name, using the Windows 10 Search feature icon:

1 Click the **Cortana** icon on the Taskbar to display the **Search box**

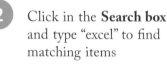

2 Click in the **Search box** and type "excel" to find matching items

3 Select the **Excel** desktop app entry in the search results to launch the application

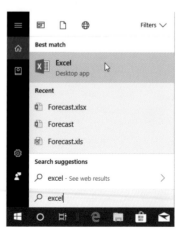

To always display the Search box, right-click the Taskbar and select Cortana, Show search box.

If you have a microphone on your system, you can use Cortana to simply ask to start applications. To check the status of Cortana:

 Click **Settings**, select **Cortana,** click **Talk to Cortana**, and ensure that Cortana is set to respond to voice commands

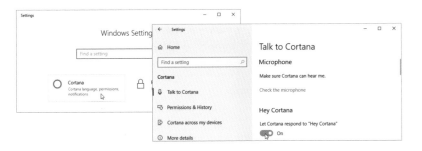

If Cortana can't hear you, or you can't hear Cortana, then click **Check the microphone** to have speech and audio settings updated.

 Say "Hey Cortana" into your system microphone to wake up your Personal Digital Assistant

Now, say "start Excel" into the microphone to launch the Excel 2019 application

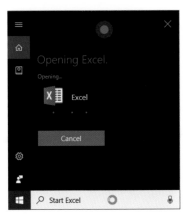

Cortana is new in Windows 10 but performance may vary by region. If Cortana is not working or enabled in your country try setting your region to "United States" in **Settings** > **Time & language** > **Region & language**.

Whichever of these techniques you use, the Excel 2019 application will be loaded and made ready to deal with your requirements.

The Office 2019 Ribbon

The menus and toolbars used in earlier versions of Excel have been replaced by the Ribbon. With this, commands are organized in logical groups, under command tabs – **Home**, **Insert**, **Page Layout**, **Formulas**, **Data**, **Review**, **View** and **Help** tabs – arranged in the order in which tasks are normally performed. When you click any of these tabs, the corresponding commands display in the Ribbon.

Hot tip

Other Office 2019 apps (Word, Access, Outlook, and PowerPoint) also have a Ribbon, which displays tabs appropriate to that particular app.

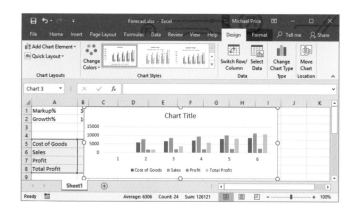

The Ribbon may also include contextual command tabs, which appear when you perform a specific task. For example, if you select some data and then click **Insert Column Chart** in the **Charts** group, chart tool tabs **Design** and **Format** are displayed.

Don't forget

The **File** tab displays the BackStage view, which provides general document file functions, plus other functions such as **Share**, **Export** and the **Excel Options**.

You can minimize the Ribbon, to use more of the space on the screen for the actual content of the spreadsheet:

 1　Click the **Ribbon Display Options** button and select **Show Tabs**

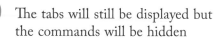 2　The tabs will still be displayed but the commands will be hidden

16

You can also choose **Auto-hide Ribbon**. Excel runs full-screen, with no tabs or commands visible. Click the top of the application to display the Ribbon.

3 The Ribbon and the commands are redisplayed as a temporary overlay whenever you click a tab, or when you use the **Alt** key shortcuts (see page 118)

Office 2019 applications offer two interfaces – Mouse or Touch, where the latter is optimized for operation with touch-enabled devices. To add this option to the Quick Access Toolbar, click the Down arrow and select **Touch/Mouse Mode**.

Touch/Mouse Mode
To enable Touch Mode:

1 Click the Down arrow on the Quick Access Toolbar, then choose the **Touch** option

2 The Ribbon displays with extra spacing between buttons

17

Exploring Excel 2019

If you are used to a previous version of Excel, you may not always know where to find the features you need. The following table lists some of the actions that you may want to carry out, and indicates the Ribbon tabs and groups where the associated commands for these actions may be found in Excel 2019:

Hot tip

Explore the Ribbon tabs and command groups in Excel 2019 to find the features that you need to carry out activities on your worksheets.

Action	Tab	Groups
Create, open, save, print, share, or export files; or change options	File	Backstage Commands – Info, New, Open, Save, Save As, Print, Share, Export, Close, Account, Options, and Feedback
Format, insert, delete, edit or find data in cells, columns, and rows	Home	Number, Styles, Cells, and Editing groups
Create tables, charts, sparklines, reports, slicers, and hyperlinks	Insert	Tables, Charts, Sparklines, Filters, and Links groups
Set page margins, page breaks, print areas, or sheet options	Page Layout	Page Setup, Scale to Fit, and Sheet Options groups
Find functions, define names, or troubleshoot formulas	Formulas	Function Library, Defined Names, and Formula Auditing groups
Import or connect to data, sort and filter data, validate data, flash fill values, or perform a what-if analysis	Data	Get External Data, Connections, Sort & Filter, and Data Tools groups
Check spelling, review and revise, and protect a sheet or workbook	Review	Proofing, Comments, and Changes groups
Change workbook views, arrange windows, freeze panes, and record macros	View	Workbook Views, Window, and Macros groups

18

Don't forget

There is a **Tell Me** text box on the Excel 2019 Ribbon where you can enter words and phrases, to quickly locate features or get help on what you want to do.

If you want to locate a particular command, you can search the list of all of the commands that are available in Excel 2019 (see next page).

...cont'd

To display the list of available commands:

1 Click the Down arrow on the Quick Access Toolbar to display its **Customize** menu (see page 17) and select the option for **More Commands**

(see page 17)

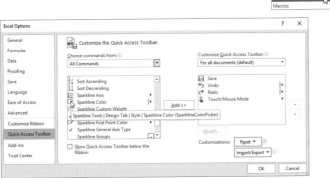

Don't forget

You can also right-click the Ribbon and select **Customize the Ribbon...** to display the list of commands and view the associated ScreenTips.

2 Click the box **Choose commands from,** and select **All Commands**

3 Scroll the list and move the mouse pointer over a command name, and the ScreenTip will indicate the tab and group containing that command

4 Some of the commands may not currently be included in any group, and so will be shown with just their name – for example, the Calculator command:

Hot tip

To list the commands that may not be currently in any group you'd select **Commands Not in the Ribbon**. You can use Customize to **Add** any of these commands to the Quick Access Toolbar or to the Ribbon.

Excel Online App

Office Online apps are touch-friendly web applications that let you create, edit and share Excel, Word, PowerPoint and OneNote files from any browser. They are free to use and can share your OneDrive storage.

1 To use the free Office Online apps, open your web browser, sign in to your Microsoft account and go to the website address **products.office.com/en-us/office-online**

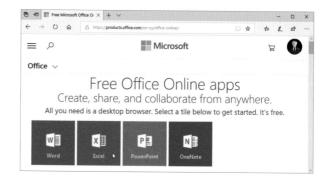

2 Select one of the Office Online app; for example, **Excel**

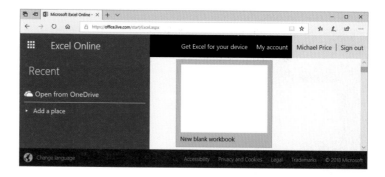

If the function you want is not provided in the Excel Online app, select **Open in Excel** to use the full desktop version, where you have Office 2019 installed.

3 Select the **New blank workbook** to begin working on a new spreadsheet

2 Begin with Excel

We start with a simple workbook, to show what's involved in entering, modifying, and formatting data, and in performing calculations. This includes ways in which Excel helps to minimize the effort. We cover printing, look at Excel Help, and discuss the various file formats associated with Excel.

22 The Excel Window

24 Create a Workbook

25 Add Data to the Worksheet

26 Build the Worksheet

28 Fill Cells

29 Complete the Worksheet

30 Format the Text

31 Format the Numbers

32 Print the Worksheet

34 Insert, Copy and Paste

35 Excel Help

36 Contextual Help

37 Excel File Formats

The Excel Window

When you launch Excel, you usually start with the Excel window displaying a blank workbook called "Book1":

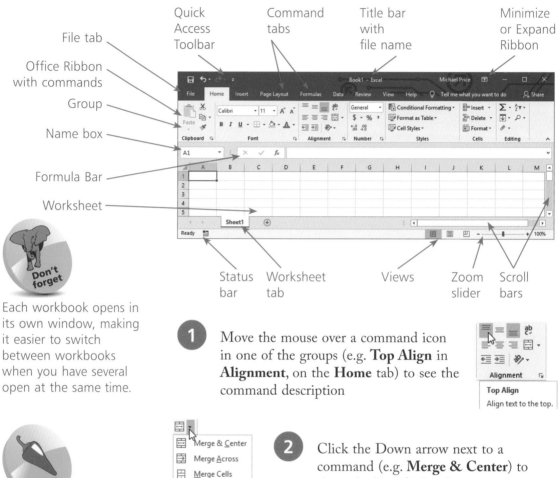

Quick Access Toolbar

Command tabs

Title bar with file name

Minimize or Expand Ribbon

File tab

Office Ribbon with commands

Group

Name box

Formula Bar

Worksheet

Status bar

Worksheet tab

Views

Zoom slider

Scroll bars

Don't forget

Each workbook opens in its own window, making it easier to switch between workbooks when you have several open at the same time.

1 Move the mouse over a command icon in one of the groups (e.g. **Top Align** in **Alignment**, on the **Home** tab) to see the command description

Top Align
Align text to the top.

Hot tip

The **Home** tab contains all the commands for basic worksheet activities, in the **Clipboard**, **Font**, **Alignment**, **Number**, **Styles**, **Cells**, and **Editing** groups.

Merge & Center
Merge Across
Merge Cells
Unmerge Cells

2 Click the Down arrow next to a command (e.g. **Merge & Center**) to show the list of related commands

3 Click the arrow by the group name (e.g. **Alignment**) to see the associated dialog box

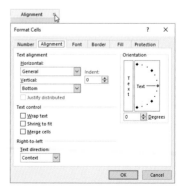

4 Select other tabs to view the other cell formatting options available

22

...cont'd

By default, Excel provides one array of data (called a worksheet) in the workbook. This is named "Sheet1". Click the **+** button to add "Sheet2", "Sheet3"; etc.

Hot tip

One worksheet is usually all you need to create a spreadsheet, but it can sometimes be convenient to organize the data into several worksheets.

Each worksheet is the equivalent of a full spreadsheet and has the potential for up to 1,048,576 x 16,384 cells, arranged in rows and columns. The rows are numbered 1, 2, 3 and onwards, up to a maximum of 1,048,576. The columns are lettered A to Z, AA to ZZ, and then AAA to XFD. This gives a maximum of 16,384 columns. The combination gives a unique reference for each cell, from A1 right up to XFD1048576. Only a very few of these cells will be visible at any one time, but any part of the worksheet can be displayed on the screen, which acts as a rectangular "porthole" onto the whole worksheet.

Beware

These are the theoretical limits for worksheets. For very large numbers of records, a database program may be a more suitable choice.

23

Use the scroll bars to reposition the screen view, or type a cell reference into the Name box; for example, ZX1024.

Don't forget

The actual number of cells shown depends on screen resolution, cell size, and display mode (e.g. with Ribbon minimized or full-screen).

See pages 44-45 for other ways to navigate through the worksheet using arrow keys, scroll functions, split views, keystrokes, the mouse, and touch.

Create a Workbook

We will start by creating a simple, personal budget workbook, to illustrate the processes involved in creating and updating your Excel spreadsheet.

1 When Excel opens, it offers a list of recent workbooks and allows you to open other workbooks. For a new workbook you could choose a template appropriate to your purpose. We'll simply select the Blank workbook, which will be named "Book1" by default, as our starting point

The Excel Start screen displays templates, and lists recent workbooks. You could select a predefined workbook template from those stored on your computer, or online at the Microsoft website.

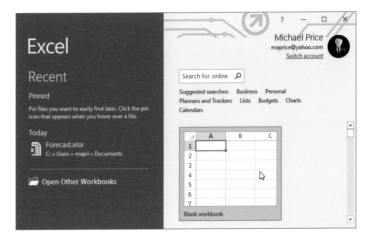

2 Type the spreadsheet title "My Personal Budget" in cell A1, and press the Down arrow, or the **Enter** key, to go to cell A2 (or just click cell A2 to select it)

Text is automatically aligned to the left of the cell; numbers are aligned to the right.

Add Data to the Worksheet

1 Continue to add text to the cells in column A, pressing the Down arrow or **Enter** to move down after each, to create labels in cells A2 to A13:

Income
Salary
Interest/dividend
Total income
Expenses
Mortgage/rent
Utilities
Groceries
Transport
Insurance
Total expenses
Savings/shortage

If the text is already available in another document, you can copy and paste the text, to save typing.

The first time you save a workbook, Save As gets called, so you can name the workbook. You should save the workbook regularly while creating or updating spreadsheets, to avoid losing your work if a system problem arises.

2 Click the **File** tab, and select **Save** (or press the **Ctrl** + **S** keyboard shortcut)

3 Select a location (in OneDrive or on your computer), then type a file name – e.g. "My Personal Budget" – and click **Save**, to add the workbook to the selected storage area

Click **Add a tag** to classify the workbook, with Tag words such as Title or Subject. If you create numerous workbooks, these details can help you manage and locate your information.

Build the Worksheet

We want to fill in the columns of data for each month of the year but first, we need an extra row after the title, for the column headings. To add a row to the worksheet:

1 Select the row (click the row number) above where you want to insert another row; e.g. select row 2

To insert multiple rows, select a block of as many rows as you need, and then click **Insert** – the new rows will be inserted above the selection. Use a similar procedure to insert one or more new columns.

26

2 Click the **Home** tab and then, in the **Cells** group, click the arrow below **Insert**, and click **Insert Sheet Rows**

3 Click cell B2 in the new row, and type "January", then press **Enter** twice, to move to B4

4 Type 3950 in cell B4, press **Enter**, type 775 in cell B5, and press **Enter** again

The = symbol signifies that what follows is a formula. This creates a formula in cell B6, to specify that Total income = Salary plus Interest/dividend. Excel automatically calculates the result and displays it in cell B6. Select the cell and look in the Formula Bar to see the formula.

5 In cell B6 type = then click in B4 and type +. Click B5 (to get **=B4+B5**) then press **Enter** to see the total appear in B6

...cont'd

6 Click cell B8, and then type the values 2250, 425, 1150, 350, and 450 (pressing the Down arrow or **Enter** after each)

7 In cell B13, type **=SUM(** and then click B8, type a period/full stop, click B12, type **)** and press **Enter**, then click B13 to see the Formula Bar contents

Some of the labels in column A appear truncated. The full label is still recorded, but the part that overlapped column B cannot be displayed, if the adjacent cell is occupied.

To change the column width to fit the contents:

1 Select the column of labels (click the letter heading)

2 On the **Home** tab, in the **Cells** group, select **Format**

3 Under **Cell Size**, select **AutoFit Column Width**

4 Alternatively, move the mouse pointer over the column boundary, and drag to manually widen or double-click to **AutoFit** to contents

You can click B13, then click the **Σ AutoSum** button in the **Editing** group on the **Home** tab. This automatically sums the adjacent cells, in this case the five cells above, giving **=SUM(B8:B12)**. See page 68 for more details of **AutoSum**.

Column width is measured in characters (assuming a standard font). The default is 8.43, but you can set any value from 0 to 255.

To change a group of columns, select the first, hold down **Shift** and select the last. For non-adjacent columns, select the first, hold down **Ctrl** and click other columns.

Fill Cells

We've typed "January", but the rest of the monthly headings can be automatically completed, using the Fill Handle:

 Select the B2 cell with the "January" heading

 Move the mouse to the bottom-right corner of the cell to see the + Fill Handle appear

 Click the Fill Handle and drag over adjacent cells to select them, then release the mouse button to fill those cells

 Change the **Auto Fill Options**, when necessary, to copy cell contents or to fill with or without formatting

Excel recognizes various entry types. If you start with "Jan", rather than "January", adjacent cells fill with "Feb", "Mar", "Apr"; etc.

 Select cell B4, and fill cells C4:G4 with a copy of B4. Repeat for B6 to C6:G6, and for B13 to C13:G13. Select the block of cells B8:B9, and fill cells C8:G9

	A	B	C	D	E	F	G	H
1	My Personal Budget							
2		Jan	Feb	Mar	Apr	May	Jun	
3	Income							
4	Salary	3950	3950	3950	3950	3950	3950	
5	Interest/dividend	775						
6	Total income	4725	3950	3950	3950	3950	3950	
7	Expenses							
8	Mortgage/rent	2250	2250	2250	2250	2250	2250	
9	Utilities	425	425	425	425	425	425	
10	Groceries	1150						
11	Transport	350						
12	Insurance	450						
13	Total expenses	4625	2675	2675	2675	2675	2675	
14	Savings/shortage							

Complete the Worksheet

 Select cell H2, and type "Period" as the heading

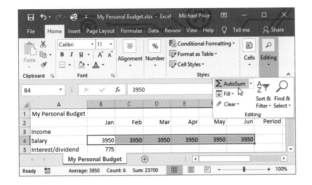

Don't forget

It is sometimes more efficient to fill a whole range of cells, then clear the ones that are not necessary.

 Select cells B4 to G4, click **AutoSum** in **Editing**, on the **Home** tab, and see that the total gets entered in cell H4

 Select cell H4, and fill cells H5 to H14, then select cell H7 and press **Delete** (no values to total)

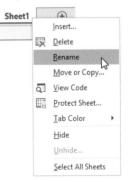

Hot tip

You can right-click the tab for Sheet1 and select **Rename**, calling it "My Personal Budget", for example.

 Select cell B14, type **=B6-B13**, then press **Enter** (type the whole formula, or select the cells to add their addresses)

Select cell B14, then drag and fill to copy the formula, for Total income-Total expenses, to the cells C14:G14

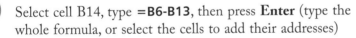

	A	B	C	D	E	F	G	H
1	My Personal Budget							
2		Jan	Feb	Mar	Apr	May	Jun	Period
3	Income							
4	Salary	3950	3950	3950	3950	3950	3950	23700
5	Interest/dividend	775						775
6	Total income	4725	3950	3950	3950	3950	3950	24475
7	Expenses							0
8	Mortgage/rent	2250	2250	2250	2250	2250	2250	13500
9	Utilities	425	425	425	425	425	425	2550
10	Groceries	1150						1150
11	Transport	350						350
12	Insurance	450						450
13	Total expenses	4625	2675	2675	2675	2675	2675	18000
14	Savings/shortage	100	1275	1275	1275	1275	1275	6475

Ready   Average: 1079.166667   Count: 6   Sum: 6475   100%

Format the Text

Although not essential for the actual function of the spreadsheet, formatting the text can make it easier to view the workbook, and make prints more readable.

There are numerous changes that you could make, but at this stage we will just make some changes to font size and styles, and to the text placement:

1 Click cell A3, press and hold **Ctrl**, and click cells A6, A7, A13 and A14, then click the arrow next to **Font Size** (in the **Home** tab **Font** group) and select size 14, then click the **Bold** font button

2 Click column label cell B2, press **Shift** and click cell H2, and then select font size 14, **Bold** for cells B2:H2, and select **Align Right** in the **Alignment** group from the **Home** tab

3 Select cell range A1 to H1, then, on the **Home** tab, select **Merge & Center** in the **Home**, **Alignment** group, and then select font size 20, **Bold** for the workbook title

Hot tip

The worksheet changes momentarily, as you move over the font sizes, showing you how the change would affect the appearance.

Beware

You may need to reapply **AutoFit** when you make changes to the font size and style for labels or to the format for data columns.

Don't forget

Whenever you make changes, click the **Save** button on the **Quick Access Toolbar** to store the workbook, so updates won't be lost.

	A	B	C	D	E	F	G	H
1				My Personal Budget				
2		Jan	Feb	Mar	Apr	May	Jun	Period
3	**Income**							
4	Salary	3950	3950	3950	3950	3950	3950	23700
5	Interest/dividend	775						775
6	**Total income**	4725	3950	3950	3950	3950	3950	24475
7	**Expenses**							
8	Mortgage/rent	2250	2250	2250	2250	2250	2250	13500
9	Utilities	425	425	425	425	425	425	2550
10	Groceries	1150						1150
11	Transport	350						350
12	Insurance	450						450
13	**Total expenses**	4625	2675	2675	2675	2675	2675	18000
14	**Savings/shortage**	100	1275	1275	1275	1275	1275	6475

My Personal Budget.xlsx - Excel   Michael Price

File   Home   Insert   Page Layout   Formulas   Data   Review   View   Help   Tell me   Share

A17

My Personal Budget

Ready   100%

Format the Numbers

To apply a specific format to numbers in your worksheet:

 1 Select the cells that you wish to reformat, and click the Down arrow in the **Number** format box

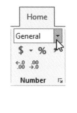

See pages 58-59 for details of the various types of formats available for numbers in cells.

2 Select **More Number Formats...** then choose – for example – **Number**, Decimal places **2**, and Negative numbers **Red**

3 Click **OK**, to apply the format change

4 Change the width of the columns to display all data (see page 27)

The **General** format isn't consistent. Decimal places vary, and Excel may apply rounding, to fit numbers in if the column is too narrow.

5 **Save** the changes

February	ruary	ıary
3950	3950	3950
567.75	567.8	568
4517.75	4518	4518
2250	2250	2250
425.04	425	425
1124.9	1125	1125
437.5	437.5	438
450	450	450
4687.44	4687	4687
-169.69	-169.7	-170

My Personal Budget.xlsx - Excel — Michael Price

	A	B	C	D	E	F	G	H	I
1			My Personal Budget						
2		Jan	Feb	Mar	Apr	May	Jun	Period	
3	Income								
4	Salary	3950.00	3950.00	3950.00	3950.00	3950.00	3950.00	23700.00	
5	Interest/dividend	775.00	567.75					1342.75	
6	Total income	4725.00	4517.75	3950.00	3950.00	3950.00	3950.00	25042.75	
7	Expenses								
8	Mortgage/rent	2250.00	2250.00	2250.00	2250.00	2250.00	2250.00	13500.00	
9	Utilities	425.00	425.04	425.00	425.00	425.00	425.00	2550.04	
10	Groceries	1150.00	1124.90					2274.90	
11	Transport	350.00	437.50					787.50	
12	Insurance	450.00	450.00					900.00	
13	Total expenses	4625.00	4687.44	2675.00	2675.00	2675.00	2675.00	20012.44	
14	Savings/shortage	100.00	169.69	1275.00	1275.00	1275.00	1275.00	5030.31	

My Personal Budget

Print the Worksheet

If you want to print only part of the data in the worksheet, select the range of cells before selecting **Print** (see page 33).

If you ever scroll past the end of the data, and accidentally click a key or the spacebar, Excel will think this is part of the worksheet data.

Press the **Zoom to Page** button to toggle between close-up and full-page view. Click the **Show Margins** button to toggle margin indicators.

1 Select the worksheet you want to print (if there's more than one in your workbook), click the **File** tab, and then choose **Print**

2 You'll see the print options, plus the print preview for your current worksheet

3 Check to see exactly what data will be printed, especially if there are more pages than you were expecting

My Personal Budget							
	Jan	Feb	Mar	Apr	May	Jun	Period
Income							
Salary	3950.00	3950.00	3950.00	3950.00	3950.00	3950.00	23700.00
Interest/dividend	775.00	567.75					1342.75
Total income	4725.00	4517.75	3950.00	3950.00	3950.00	3950.00	25042.75
Expenses							
Mortgage/rent	2250.00	2250.00	2250.00	2250.00	2250.00	2250.00	13500.00
Utilities	425.00	425.04	425.00	425.00	425.00	425.00	2550.04
Groceries	1150.00	1124.90					2274.90
Transport	350.00	437.50					787.50
Insurance	450.00	450.00					900.00
Total expenses	4625.00	4687.44	2675.00	2675.00	2675.00	2675.00	20012.44
Savings/shortage	100.00	169.69	1275.00	1275.00	1275.00	1275.00	5030.31

Excel will select a print area that will include all the cells that appear to have data in them (including blanks), and as a result could select a larger print area than you might have anticipated. For example, you may have scrolled down the spreadsheet and used some cells to carry out some preliminary calculations. These would automatically get included in the print.

4 Click the **Printer** button to change the printer if desired

5 Click the **Settings** button to choose between the active sheet, the entire workbook, or just the current selection

6 Other **Print** settings let you choose the pages to print and to specify duplex, orientation, and paper size

If there is a print area defined, Excel will only print that part of the worksheet. If you don't want to limit the print this time, select **Ignore Print Area**.

7 Specify the number of copies, then click the **Print** button to send the document to the printer

Copies: 2

For printing part of the worksheet, you can preset the print area:

 1 Select the range of cells that you normally want printed

2 Select the **Page Layout** tab, click the **Print Area** button in the **Page Setup** group, and select **Set Print Area**

If you are sure that the default print settings are what you require, you can add the **Quick Print** button to the Quick Access Toolbar (see page 119) and use this to print immediately.

		Jan	Feb	Mar	Apr	May	Jun	Period
1	**My Personal Budget**							
2		Jan	Feb	Mar	Apr	May	Jun	Period
3	**Income**							
4	Salary	3950.00	3950.00	3950.00	3950.00	3950.00	3950.00	23700.00
5	Interest/dividend	775.00	567.75					1342.75
6	**Total income**	4725.00	4517.75	3950.00	3950.00	3950.00	3950.00	25042.75
7	**Expenses**							
8	Mortgage/rent	2250.00	2250.00	2250.00	2250.00	2250.00	2250.00	13500.00
9	Utilities	425.00	425.04	425.00	425.00	425.00	425.00	2550.04
10	Groceries	1150.00	1124.90					2274.90
11	Transport	350.00	437.50					787.50
12	Insurance	450.00	450.00					900.00
13	**Total expenses**	4625.00	4687.44	2675.00	2675.00	2675.00	2675.00	20012.44
14	**Savings/shortage**	100.00	169.69	1275.00	1275.00	1275.00	1275.00	5030.31

Ready   Average: 3834.484255   Count: 65   Sum: 180220.76

Insert, Copy and Paste

You can rearrange the contents of the worksheet, or add new data, by inserting rows or columns and copying cells. For example, to add an additional six months of information:

 Click in column H, press **Shift**, and click in column M

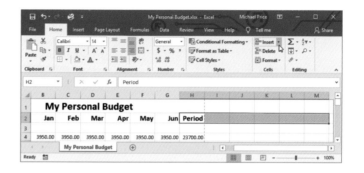

Hot tip

Select the "Jun" month header cell **G2** and use the Fill Handle (see page 28) to fill cells **H2:M2**, adding "Jul" to "Dec".

---

2 Select the **Home** tab, click the arrow next to **Insert** in the **Cells** group, and choose **Insert Sheet Columns**

3 Select range G4:G14, and then click the **Copy** button

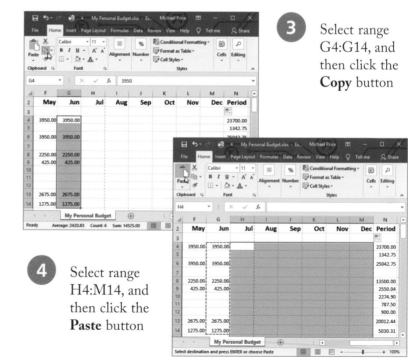

Hot tip

After copying the data range, change the formula in N4 from =**SUM(B4:G4)** to =**SUM(B4:M4)**, and copy the formula into cells N5:N6 and N8:N14.

4 Select range H4:M14, and then click the **Paste** button

Excel Help

There are two ways to get help when using the Excel app – you can seek specific help using the **Tell Me** box, or call upon the online **Help** facility for general assistance:

1   Click the **Tell Me** box on the Tab bar, then type the topic you want help with; for example, "insert rows"

2   You'll see **Best Match**, and four other **Actions**. Review the most appropriate of the responses

3   Alternatively, press the **F1** key on your keyboard to display the main Help facility

This always starts up with worksheet basics such as **Get started** and **Formatting**.

4   Select any entry to expand that topic and find links to subtopics

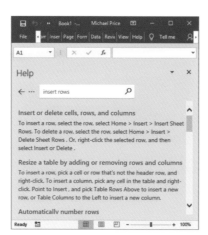

5   To get specific help on your chosen topic, type "insert rows" into the Search box then click the search button

6   You'd get the same results if you selected the **Get Help on "insert rows"** at the foot of the **Tell Me** results list

7   Now, choose a link (highlighted in blue) from the list for detailed help on that related topic

Hot tip

As well as Office Help, **Tell Me** uses **Smart Lookup** that finds information on your search term from various online sources, including Wikipedia.

Don't forget

You can also access the Excel Help facility if you select the **Help** tab then click the **Help** icon.

Contextual Help

You do not always need to search for help – you can get specific information on a particular command or operation via ScreenTips:

1 Open a command tab, then move the mouse pointer over a command in one of the groups to reveal the ScreenTip

Don't forget

Some ScreenTips have just a brief description, plus a keyboard shortcut, where appropriate. Other ScreenTips are more expansive.

2 If you see the **Help** icon at the foot of the ScreenTip, click that entry or press **F1** (with the ScreenTip still visible) to see the relevant article

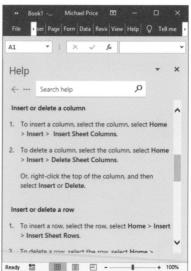

3 View the video, or scroll down to see more of the article

Hot tip

You can still use the Search box to locate additional articles on the topic of interest.

Excel File Formats

When you save your workbook in Excel 2019 (see page 25) it uses the default file type **.xlsx**. To save your workbook in a format for previous versions of Excel:

1 Click the **File** tab and select **Save As**, then select the location; e.g. **Documents**

A workbook created in an earlier version of Excel will remain as file type **.xls** if modified – unless you choose to save it in Excel 2019 file format.

2 Click the box for **Save as type**, and select the **Excel 97–2003 Workbook (*.xls)** file type

Save As	
« mapri › Documents	Search Documents

File name: My Personal Budget.xlsx

Save as type: Excel Workbook (*.xlsx)

Excel Workbook (*.xlsx)
Excel Macro-Enabled Workbook (*.xlsm)
Excel Binary Workbook (*.xlsb)
Excel 97-2003 Workbook (*.xls)
CSV UTF-8 (Comma delimited) (*.csv)
XML Data (*.xml)
Single File Web Page (*.mht;*.mhtml)
Web Page (*.htm;*.html)
Excel Template (*.xltx)
Excel Macro-Enabled Template (*.xltm)
Excel 97-2003 Template (*.xlt)
Text (Tab delimited) (*.txt)
Unicode Text (*.txt)
XML Spreadsheet 2003 (*.xml)
Microsoft Excel 5.0/95 Workbook (*.xls)
CSV (Comma delimited) (*.csv)
Formatted Text (Space delimited) (*.prn)
Text (Macintosh) (*.txt)
Text (MS-DOS) (*.txt)
CSV (Macintosh) (*.csv)
CSV (MS-DOS) (*.csv)
DIF (Data Interchange Format) (*.dif)
SYLK (Symbolic Link) (*.slk)
Excel Add-in (*.xlam)
Excel 97-2003 Add-in (*.xla)
PDF (*.pdf)
XPS Document (*.xps)
Strict Open XML Spreadsheet (*.xlsx)
OpenDocument Spreadsheet (*.ods)

You can save and open files in the **Strict Open XML Spreadsheet (*.xlsx)** file format, which allows you to read and write ISO8601 dates to resolve a leap year issue for the year 1900 (see page 59).

3 Change the file name, if desired, and click the **Save** button

Save As	
« mapri › Documents	Search Documents

File name: My Personal Budget.xls

Save as type: Excel 97-2003 Workbook (*.xls)

Authors: Michael Price   Tags: Add a tag

☐ Save Thumbnail

˅ Browse Folders   Tools ▾   Save   Cancel

4 You'll now see two copies of the workbook, with different file types and icons

Documents	– □ ×
File Home Share View	
« Users › mapri › Documents	Search Do...

Contacts
Creative Cloud Files
Desktop
Documents
Downloads

My Personal Budget.xls   My Personal Budget.xlsx

7 items

The file icons indicate the specific file type, but to see the file extensions, select the **View** tab in File Explorer and click **File name extensions** in the **Show/hide** group.

☐ Item check boxes
☑ File name extensions
☐ Hidden items
Hide selected items

Show/hide

...cont'd

You can save your workbooks in a variety of other file formats, which will make it easier to share information with others who may not have the same applications software.

 Click the **File** tab, select **Save As** and choose the format you want to use; for example, **CSV (Comma delimited)**

 You may be warned of potential conflicts. For example, you should use negative signs or brackets in numbers rather than the red code, since colors are removed

Text and number formatting will be removed, and only the current worksheet is saved

If there's more than one worksheet in your workbook, you'll need to select and save each one in turn to a separate file.

Hot tip

You can also display the **Save As** dialog by pressing the **F12** key.

Don't forget

Text (Tab delimited) or **CSV (Comma delimited)** formats are often used to exchange information, since most applications will support these formats.

3 Manage Data

This chapter introduces navigation tools, commands, and facilities, to enable you to find your way around and work with large spreadsheets. It shows how existing data can be imported into Excel, to avoid having to retype information.

40 Use Existing Data

42 Import Data

44 Navigate the Worksheet

46 Scroll with the Wheel Mouse

47 Keystrokes and Touch

48 Sort Rows

49 Find Entries

50 Filter Information

52 Remove Duplicate Entries

53 Check Spelling

54 Freeze Headers and Labels

55 Hide Columns or Rows

56 Protect a Worksheet

Use Existing Data

To identify the file types that can be opened directly in Excel:

 Within a blank workbook/worksheet, select the **File** tab and click **Open** (or press **Ctrl + O**) and select the file location; e.g. **Documents**

 Click the file type box, alongside the **File name** box

If the information you want to add to a workbook already exists in another application, you may be able to import it into Excel and use it without having to retype the data, as long as you can prepare it in a suitable file format.

All Excel Files	∨
All Files	
All Excel Files	
Excel Files	
All Web Pages	
XML Files	
Text Files	
All Data Sources	
Access Databases	
Query Files	
dBase Files	
Microsoft Excel 4.0 Macros	
Microsoft Excel 4.0 Workbooks	
Worksheets	
Workspaces	
Templates	
Add-ins	
Toolbars	
SYLK Files	
Data Interchange Format	
Backup Files	
OpenDocument Spreadsheet	

All Excel Files (*.xl*;*.xlsx;*.xlsm; ∨
All Files (*.*)
All Excel Files (*.xl*;*.xlsx;*.xlsm;*.xlsb;*.xlam;*.xltx;*.xltm;*.xls;*.xlt;*.htm;*.html;*.mht;*.mhtml;*.xml;*.xla;*.xlm;*.xlw;*.odc;*.ods)
Excel Files (*.xl*;*.xlsx;*.xlsm;*.xlsb;*.xlam;*.xltx;*.xltm;*.xls;*.xla;*.xlt;*.xlm;*.xlw)
All Web Pages (*.htm;*.html;*.mht;*.mhtml)
XML Files (*.xml)
Text Files (*.prn;*.txt;*.csv)
All Data Sources (*.odc;*.udl;*.dsn;*.mdb;*.mde;*.accdb;*.accde;*.dbc;*.iqy;*.dqy;*.rqy;*.oqy;*.cub;*.atom;*.atomsvc)
Access Databases (*.mdb;*.mde;*.accdb;*.accde)
Query Files (*.iqy;*.dqy;*.oqy;*.rqy)
dBase Files (*.dbf)
Microsoft Excel 4.0 Macros (*.xlm;*.xla)
Microsoft Excel 4.0 Workbooks (*.xlw)
Worksheets (*.xlsx;*.xlsm;*.xlsb;*.xls)
Workspaces (*.xlw)
Templates (*.xltx;*.xltm;*.xlt)
Add-ins (*.xlam;*.xla;*.xll)
Toolbars (*.xlb)
SYLK Files (*.slk)
Data Interchange Format (*.dif)
Backup Files (*.xlk;*.bak)
OpenDocument Spreadsheet (*.ods)

 Identify a file type supported by the other application (e.g. **Text** or **CSV**) and then click **Cancel** for the moment

 Extract data from the other application, as that file type

For example, you might have a number of MP3 tracks created by transferring your CD collection to the hard drive.

Excel uses features of File Explorer in Windows 10. If you select the box **File name extensions** on the **View** tab in File Explorer (see page 37), you'll see the extended details for the supported file types.

Each file stores particulars of the music it contains, including title, album, artist, composer, recording date, quality (the bit rate used for conversion), genre; etc. This information is stored in the music file in the form of MP3 tags.

Applications such as **Mp3tag (mp3tag.de/en/download.html)** can scan the MP3 files and extract the tags, allowing you to make changes or corrections to the details that are saved.

1 Click **File, Change directory** to specify your Music folder

Mp3tag will scan all your music files and display the tag details.

Details of the music are downloaded from the internet when you transfer the tracks to the hard disk, using an application like Windows Media Player. It also records the settings used for the conversion to MP3 format.

2 Click **Edit, Select all files**, then click **File, Export...** to output these details

3 Choose the output file type – for example, **csv** – and click **OK**

4 Click **No** to avoid opening the **mp3tag.csv** file in Excel for the moment

5 Use Notepad to view the contents of this file, which you will find in the Music folder that you selected

The first line gives field names for the selection of tags exported, and each subsequent line relates to one MP3 file with its values for each of the data fields.

Import Data

1 Within Excel, select **Open** on the **File** tab, then **Browse** to select the data file you exported and click **Open**

Select the file type you used to export data from the application, and follow the prompts. This example shows the process for CSV text files.

2 This launches the **Text Import Wizard**, which assesses your file and chooses the appropriate settings – in this case, Delimited. Click the box to confirm your data has headers

Don't forget

Check the settings applied by the import wizard, and make any changes that are required for your particular files.

3 Adjust the delimiters and the text qualifier for your file, if any changes are needed, and preview the effect

4 Review each column in turn; decide whether you want to skip that data item, change the data format, or accept the suggested format

The **General** data format is the most flexible. It interprets numerical values as dates, leaving all other values as text.

5 Click the **Finish** button to load the data into your Excel worksheet, with lines as rows and data items as columns

6 Select **Save As**, from the **File** tab, change the file type to "Excel Workbook", provide a name such as **Music_List** and press the **Save** button

Be sure to save the worksheet as an Excel Workbook, not as a text file, and/or provide a new name to avoid the possibility of overwriting the original import file.

Navigate the Worksheet

If you've transferred information from an existing application and then find yourself with some rather large worksheets, you'll welcome the variety of ways Excel provides to move around the worksheet.

Arrow Keys

Ctrl + Arrow key takes you to the edge of the worksheet, if the active cell is the last occupied cell in the direction of the arrow.

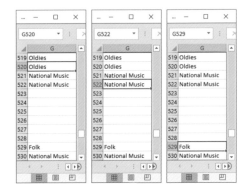

1 Press an arrow key to move the point of focus (the active cell) one cell per tap, in the direction of that arrow

2 Hold down the **Ctrl** key and press the arrow key, to move to the start or end of a range of data (an adjacent set of occupied cells)

When the **Scroll Lock** is selected, the words "Scroll Lock" are displayed on the status bar and, if present, the **Scroll Lock** light on the keyboard is turned on.

3 To select cells while scrolling to the start or end of a range, hold down the **Ctrl** and **Shift** keys and press the arrow key

4 Press **Ctrl + Shift + (arrow)** again to extend the selection

Scroll Lock

Press **Scroll Lock** to turn on scroll locking. This changes the actions of the arrow keys.

1 The arrow keys move the window view up or down one row, or sideways one column, depending which arrow key you use

2 The active cell remains unchanged

Ctrl + Arrow key shifts the view vertically, by the depth of the window, or horizontally, by the width of the window, depending on the arrow key you choose.

44

Scroll Bars

1 Click the vertical scroll arrows, to move one row up or down

2 Click above or below the scroll box, to move the view a window's depth up or down

3 Click the horizontal scroll arrows, to move one column to the left or right, or click on the horizontal scroll bar to move the window width left or right

4 Click one of the scroll boxes. Excel displays the row number or column letter as you drag the scroll box

The sizes of the scroll boxes are based on the ratios of visible data to total data, and their positions are the relative vertical and horizontal locations of the visible area within the worksheet.

Split View

You can split the window, so you can scroll separate parts of the worksheet in two or four panes, independently.

1 Select the cell where you want to apply the split, select the **View** tab and click **Split** in the **Window** group

To reposition either the horizontal or vertical split divider, move the mouse pointer over the bar and drag using the doubled-headed arrow. To remove one or other divider, just double-click the bar.

2 The worksheet now has four panes with separate scroll bars

45

Scroll with the Wheel Mouse

 Rotate the wheel forward or back, to scroll down or up a few lines at a time

2 To change the amount scrolled, open the Control Panel and select **Mouse**, then click the **Wheel** tab and change the number of lines, or select **One screen at a time**

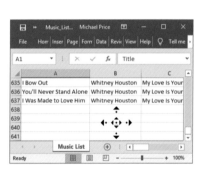

Devices
Bluetooth, printers, mouse

3 You can also carry out Horizontal Scrolling, if the mouse wheel can be tilted left or right

Continuous Scroll

 Hold down the wheel button, then drag the pointer away from the origin mark, in the direction you want to scroll

2 Release the wheel when you reach the required position

Hands-free Scroll

1 To scroll automatically, click and release the wheel button, then move the mouse in the required direction

2 The further away from the origin mark you place the mouse pointer, the faster the scrolling

3 To slow down scrolling, move the mouse pointer back, closer to the origin mark

 To stop automatic scrolling, click any mouse button

Keystrokes and Touch

The use of the arrow keys for navigation is covered on page 44. Here are some additional keyboard shortcuts:

End Key

With **Scroll Lock** off, press **End**, then press one of the arrow keys, to move to the edge of the data region

With **Scroll Lock** on, press **End** to move to the cell in the lower-right corner of the window

Ctrl + **End** moves to the last used cell (end of lowest used row)

Ctrl + **Shift** + **End** extends the selection to the last used cell

Home Key

With **Scroll Lock** off, press **Home** to move to the beginning of the current row

With **Scroll Lock** on, press **Home** to move to the cell in the upper-left corner of the window

Ctrl + **Home** moves to the beginning of the worksheet

Ctrl + **Shift** + **Home** extends the selection to the beginning

Page Down Key

Page Down moves one screen down in the worksheet

Alt + **Page Down** moves one screen to the right

Ctrl + **Page Down** moves to the next sheet in the workbook

Ctrl + **Shift** + **Page Down** selects the current and next sheet

Page Up Key

Page Up moves one screen up in the worksheet

Alt + **Page Up** moves one screen to the left

Ctrl + **Page Up** moves to the previous sheet in the workbook

Ctrl + **Shift** + **Page Up** selects the current and previous sheet

Tab Key

Tab moves one cell to the right in the worksheet

Shift + **Tab** moves to the previous cell in the worksheet

If you have a tablet PC or a touch-enabled monitor, you can easily scroll through the worksheet by dragging the screen horizontally or vertically.

Swipe the screen to move across the worksheet by a larger amount.

You can also use touch gestures to select ranges and autofill cells.

Display Excel **Help** (see page 35) for more information about using touch gestures in Excel.

Sort Rows

If you are looking for particular information, and don't know exactly where it appears in the worksheet, you can use Excel commands to help locate the items.

Custom Sort (see page 82) allows you to sort the worksheet by several fields – "Artists" and "Albums", for example.

 Click the column that contains the information and select **Sort & Filter** from the **Home** tab's **Editing** group

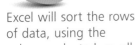

Excel will sort the rows of data, using the column selected, so all the related data will stay together.

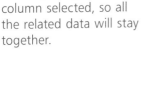 Choose **Sort A to Z** (or **Sort Z to A**, if the required information would be towards the end of the list)

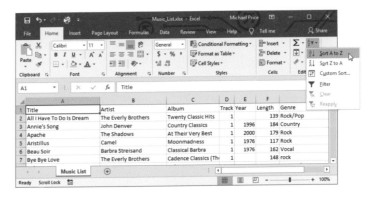

Excel provides a more structured way of handling a range of data like this, with the Excel Table – see pages 72-73.

 Scroll through the list (using the navigation techniques described on pages 44-45) to locate the relevant entries

Click **Don't Save** when you close the workbook, to keep the original order

Find Entries

If you'd rather not change the sequence of the rows, you can use the **Find** command to locate appropriate entries.

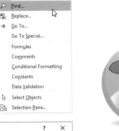

1 Click the column with the information, choose **Find & Select** from the **Editing** group on the **Home** tab, then click **Find** (or press **Ctrl + F**)

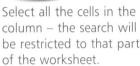
Don't forget

Select all the cells in the column – the search will be restricted to that part of the worksheet.

2 Click the **Options** button, if necessary (Excel remembers the last setting)

3 Specify a word or phrase, and select the options. For example, within the **Sheet**, search **By Columns**, look in **Values**, then click **Find Next**

	A	B	C	D	E	F	G	
54	I'll Remember	Madonna	Something to Remember	2	1995	264	Dance	6.
55	Man of Mystery	The Shadows	At Their Very Best	2	2000	121	Rock	2.
56	Monday, Monday	Spirit	Greatest Hits	2	1998	206	Easy Listening	4.
57	Never Say Goodbye	Hayley Westenra	Pure	2	2004	193	Classical	4.
58	Nine Million Bicycles	Katie Melua	Piece by Piece	2	2005	195	Rock	4.
59	Perhaps Love	John Denver	Country Classics	2	1996	179	Country	4.
60	Rhayader	Camel	The Snow Goose	2	1975	182	Rock	4.

4 Keep selecting **Find Next**, to locate each subsequent matching entry

Hot tip

You can include case in the check, and you can require a full match with the entire cell contents.

5 You can click **Find All** to get a list of the cell addresses and values for all of the matching entries in the worksheet

Book	Sheet	Name	Cell	Value
Music_List.xlsx	Music List		$A$57	Never Say Goodbye
Music_List.xlsx	Music List		$A$185	Goodbye Love [Remix]
Music_List.xlsx	Music List		$A$265	Someone Said Goodbye
Music_List.xlsx	Music List		$A$507	Goodbye Again
Music_List.xlsx	Music List		$K$57	02 Never Say Goodbye.mp3

8 cell(s) found

Filter Information

The **Filter** part of the **Sort & Filter** command can be very helpful in assessing the information you have imported, because it allows you to concentrate on particular sections of the data.

1 Select all the data (for example, click in the data region, press **Ctrl + End**, then press **Shift + Ctrl + Home**)

Don't forget

If there's only one block of data, you can press **Ctrl + A** to select all the cells in the worksheet.

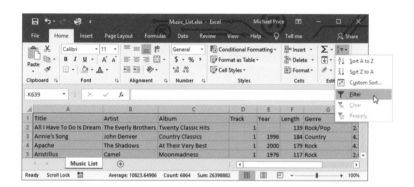

2 Select **Sort & Filter** from the **Home** tab, **Editing** group, and then click the **Filter** command

Arrow boxes will now appear in each column alongside the headings.

3 Click the arrow box in any column heading, to see a list of unique column values

Hot tip

If you want just a few entries, clear the **(Select All)** box, which clears all the boxes, then just reselect the ones you want.

4 Clear the boxes for unwanted values, to leave those you want to view; e.g. artists with guest artists

5 Click **OK** to display only those selected entries

In this example, we see tracks where Celine Dion is featured with various guests. This can make it harder to produce listings by artist, so we will show one way to reposition this information.

Hot tip

Having consistent values
for the entries makes
it much easier to sort
and organize your
information.

6 Add a **Comments** column and transfer the guest artist information to that column, leaving just the main artist

7 Click the arrow button in the column heading again, to see the list of unique values once more

You can use Filter to assess the entries in your list; for example, to find those that have incomplete information.

Don't forget

To remove filters from all columns, reselect the **Filter** command from the **Home** tab, **Editing** group. All entries will then be displayed.

1 Select the **Genre** column and **Filter** for **Blanks**

2 You'll see the list of entries that have no Genre details, so you can update them as necessary

51

Remove Duplicate Entries

A duplicate entry is where all values in the row are an exact match for all the values in another row.

To find and remove duplicate values:

1 Select the range of cells

52

2 Select the **Data** tab, then, from the **Data Tools** group, click **Remove Duplicates**

3 Click **Select All**, to ensure all columns are checked, though you might choose to clear the boxes for values such as **Filename** or **Path**

4 Clear the box for **My data has headers**, if you suspect these may be repeated

5 Click **OK** to detect and delete the duplicates

A message is displayed, indicating how many duplicate values were removed and how many unique values remain.

6 The action is complete, so click **OK** to end

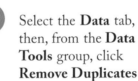

Check Spelling

A spelling check is sometimes a useful way to assess the contents of some sections of your worksheet.

1 Select the relevant parts: for example, click the **Title** column, press and hold **Ctrl**, then click the **Album** and **Genre** columns in turn

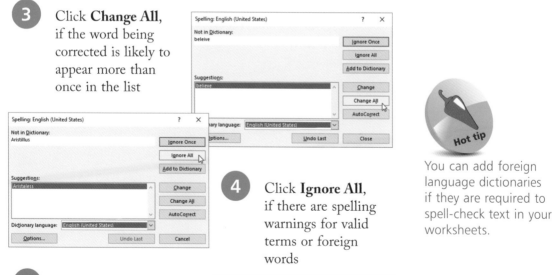

Select columns of data that contain text values that need spell-checking.

2 Select the **Review** tab, then click the **Spelling** command in the **Proofing** group (or press **F7**)

3 Click **Change All**, if the word being corrected is likely to appear more than once in the list

4 Click **Ignore All**, if there are spelling warnings for valid terms or foreign words

Hot tip

You can add foreign language dictionaries if they are required to spell-check text in your worksheets.

5 Click **OK** when the check is completed and all required changes have been applied

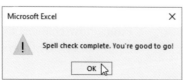

Freeze Headers and Labels

When you navigate a worksheet, column headings and row labels will move off screen, making it more difficult to identify the data elements. To keep these visible, start by clicking on the worksheet:

 Click the cell below the headings and to the right of the labels (e.g. with one row and one column, choose cell B2)

There are predefined options for a single heading row, or a single label column.

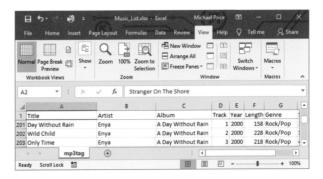

 Select the **View** tab and click the **Freeze Panes** command, from the **Window** group

 Choose an option from the list; for example, **Freeze Top Row**

Don't forget

You can now scroll down and the headings stay visible. Similarly, if you scroll across, the row labels now stay visible.

The first entry in **Freeze Panes** now changes to the undo option, **Unfreeze Panes**

Beware

You cannot freeze rows and columns when you share your workbooks for collaborative changes.

Hide Columns or Rows

To make it easier to view particular portions of the worksheet, you can tell Excel not to display certain columns or rows:

1 Select the columns or rows that you want to hide. To select non-adjacent columns, select the first column, hold down **Ctrl**, then select subsequent columns

Hot tip

You can also right-click a selected group of rows or columns, and then click **Hide** or **Unhide** from the context menu that appears.

2 Select the **Home** tab, then click **Format** in the **Cells** group

3 Select **Hide & Unhide**, then click **Hide Columns** or **Hide Rows**, as required

Hot tip

You cannot cancel the selection of a cell, or range of cells in a non-adjacent selection, without canceling the entire selection.

55

To redisplay the hidden columns or hidden rows:

1 Select the columns either side of the hidden columns, or select the rows above and below the hidden rows

2 Open the **Hide & Unhide** menu and select **Unhide Columns** or **Unhide Rows**, as appropriate

Don't forget

A column or row also becomes hidden if you change its column width or row height to zero. The **Unhide** command will reveal columns and rows hidden in this way.

Protect a Worksheet

Don't forget

Once you've set up your worksheet the way you want, you can lock it, to protect it from being accidentally changed.

Beware

There's a greater need to protect workbooks in Excel 2019 where you use storage on OneDrive that is accessible to other users.

Hot tip

When you protect the sheet, the command changes to **Unprotect Sheet**, to allow you to reverse the process.

1 Select any column (**Genre**, for example) that you might want to update

2 On the **Home** tab, select **Format** from the **Cells** group, then click **Format Cells...**

3 To protect the remaining part of the worksheet, select the **Review** tab and click **Protect Sheet** in the **Changes** group

4 Ensure that all users are allowed to select locked and unlocked cells, then click **OK**

5 You can edit cells in the chosen columns (e.g. **Genre**)

6 You get an error message if you attempt to edit other cells (e.g. in the **Title** column)

4 Formulas and Functions

Various formats for numbers are explained, and options for referencing cell locations are reviewed. These provide the basis for an introduction to functions and formulas, beginning with operators and calculation sequence, including formula errors and cell comments.

58 Number Formats

60 Text Formats

61 Relative References

62 Absolute References

63 Name References

64 Operators

65 Calculation Sequence

66 Functions

68 AutoSum

69 Formula Errors

70 Add Comments

Number Formats

The cells in the worksheet contain values, in the form of numbers or text characters. The associated cell formats control how the contents are displayed.

Number Format	Displayed as	Notes
1		
2 General	3.33333	
3 Number	3.33	Two decimal places
4 Currency	$3.33	$ symbol
5 Accountancy	$ 3.33	$ symbol alignment
6 Percentage	333.33%	1.00 equivalent to 100%
7 Fraction	3 1/3	
8 Scientific	3.33E+00	Number times power of 10
9 Text	3.33333	Left aligned, as typed
10 Special	000-00-0003	Social Security Number

Don't forget

The default format is **General**, which is based on the cell contents. Use **Number** when you need decimal places, and **Currency** or **Accounting** for monetary values. The **Special** format is for structured numbers; e.g. zip or postal codes.

Cells B2 to B10 above all contain the same value (3.33333) but each cell has a different format, which changes the way the number appears on the worksheet. To set the number format:

1 Select the cell or cells, then click the **Home** tab and choose a format from the **Number** group, or click the arrow next to **Number** for more options

2 For greater control of the formats, such as how negative numbers appear, select **More Number Formats** from the drop-down menu and choose a category and attributes from the **Format Cells** panel

Don't forget

The values can be typed directly into the cells, imported from another application (see pages 42-43), or created by a formula.

Format Cells

Number | Alignment | Font | Border | Fill | Protection

Category:
General
Number
Currency
Accounting
Date
Time
Percentage
Fraction
Scientific
Text
Special
Custom

Sample
3.33

Decimal places: 2

☐ Use 1000 Separator (,)

Negative numbers:
-1234.10
1234.10
(1234.10)
(1234.10)

Number is used for general display of numbers. Currency and Accounting offer specialized formatting for monetary value.

OK | Cancel

...cont'd

Date and **Time** are also number formats, but in this case the number is taken as the days since a base point in time.

Cells B3 to B6 are formatted as **Date** or **Time**. The same numbers are shown in cells B8 to B11, formatted as **General**. This shows that day 1 is January 1st 1900, day 42314 is November 6th 2015, while day 42321 is a week later. Decimals indicate part days.

To set or change the date or time format:

1 Open **Format Cells**, select the **Number** tab, and click **Date** or **Time** to see the list of format options

2 Choose a format option and click **OK**, or click **Custom** to see other time and date formatting options

Because dates and times are stored as numbers, you can use them in formulas and calculations.

Some of the formats depend on the specific country and locations defined in the Windows regional options, found in the Control Panel.

When dates are based on 1/1/1900, day 60 is incorrectly treated as February 29th 1900. In Excel 2019 this can be resolved using the **Strict Open XML** file format (see page 37).

Text Formats

Excel recognizes cells containing text, such as header and label cells, and gives them the **General** format, with default text format settings (left-aligned, and using the standard font). You can view or change the format for such cells:

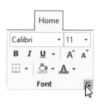

1 Select a cell or a range of cells, then click the bottom right-hand corner button on the **Font** group to open the **Format Cells** panel

2 Select the **Font** tab to adjust the font, style, size, or color

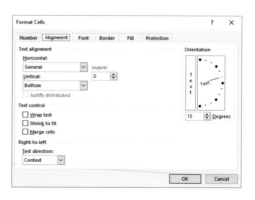

3 Select the **Alignment** tab and change the text controls, alignment, or orientation settings

Relative References

A cell could contain a formula, rather than an actual value. Excel performs the calculation the formula represents, and displays the result as the value for that cell. For example:

In this worksheet, cell D3 shows the amount spent on DVDs (price times quantity), and it is calculated as **=B3*C3**.

The formulas for D4 and D5 are created by copying and pasting D3. The cell references in the formula are relative to the position of the cell containing them, and are automatically updated for the new location.

A cell reference in this form is known as a "relative reference", and this is the normal type of reference used in worksheets.

The results of formulas can be used in other formulas, so the total in cell D6 is calculated as **=D3+D4+D5**.

The sales tax in cell D7 is calculated as **=D6*B7**. Note that B7 is displayed as a value of 7.5%, the cell format being **Percentage**. The actual value stored in the cell is 0.075.

The worksheet could have used a constant value instead, such as **=D6*7.5/100** or **=D6*7.5%**. However, having the value stored in a cell makes it easier to adapt the worksheet when rates change. It also helps when the value is used more than once.

The shipping cost in cell D8 is a stored constant.

The final calculation in the worksheet is the total cost in cell D9, which is calculated as **=D6+D7+D8**.

The cells hold formulas as stored values, but it is the results that normally get displayed. To switch between results and formulas, press **Ctrl + `** (the grave accent key), or select the **Formulas** tab and click **Show Formulas**.

The value B7 is a relative cell reference, like the others, but this may not be the best option. See page 62 for the alternative, the absolute cell reference.

Absolute References

Assume that calculation of the sales tax per line item is required. The value in cell E3 for the DVDs product would be **=D3*B7**.

To fix the column, place **$** before the column letter. Likewise, to fix the row, put **$** before the row number. The other part of the reference will change when the formula is copied.

You might be tempted to copy this formula down into cells E4 and E5, but, as you see above, the results would be incorrect, giving zero values, because the relative reference B7 would be incremented to B8 and then B9, both of which are empty cells. The answer is to fix the reference to B7, so that it doesn't change when the formula is copied. To indicate this, you edit the formula, to place a $ symbol in front of the row and column addresses.

Select a cell reference in a formula, and press F4 to cycle between relative, absolute, and mixed cell references.

=ABS(B7)
=ABS($B$7)
=ABS(B$7)
=ABS($B7)

Copy this formula down into cells E4 and E5. The reference **$B$7** doesn't change, so the results are correct. This form of cell reference is known as an "absolute reference". A cell reference with only part of the address fixed, such as **$D3** or **D$3**, would be known as a "mixed reference".

Name References

Names provide a different way to refer to cells in formulas. To create a name for a cell or cell range:

1 Select the cell, or the group of cells you want to name

2 Click the Name box, on the left of the Formula Bar, and type the name you'll be using to refer to the selection, then press **Enter**

Sales_tax

3 Define any additional named cells or ranges that you need

4 Click the **Formulas** tab and select the **Name Manager**, in the **Defined Names** group, to view names in the workbook

Name	Value	Refers To	Scope	Comment
Products	{"64.75";"9.80";"23.97"}	=Sheet1!$D$3:$D$5	Workbook	
Rate1	{...}	=90%	Workbook	
Rate2	{...}	=80%	Workbook	
Rate3	{...}	=70%	Workbook	
Sales_tax	7.50%	=Sheet1!$B$7	Workbook	

Names create absolute references to cells or ranges in the current worksheet. They can be used in formulas and, when these are copied, the references will not be incremented.

	Product	Price	Quantity	Amount	Sales Tax	Discounted Amounts		
3	DVDs	12.95	5	=B3*C3	=D3*Sales_tax	=$D3*Rate1	=$D3*Rate2	=$D3*Rate3
4	Notepads	2.45	4	=B4*C4	=D4*Sales_tax	=$D4*Rate1	=$D4*Rate2	=$D4*Rate3
5	Books	7.99	3	=B5*C5	=D5*Sales_tax	=$D5*Rate1	=$D5*Rate2	=$D5*Rate3
6				=D3+D4+D5				
7	Sales tax	0.075		=D6*Sales_tax				
8	Shipping			4.95				

Don't forget

Names must start with a letter, underscore, or backslash. They can contain letters, numbers, periods/full stops, and underscores, but not spaces, and case is ignored. Their maximum length is 255 characters.

Hot tip

Names can be defined for a cell, for a range or group of cells, or for constants and functions.

Beware

You cannot use certain names, such as "R1", "R2", "R3", since these are actual cell references. You must specify non-ambiguous names, such as "Rate1", "Rate2", "Rate3"; etc.

Operators

The formulas shown so far have used several operators (+, *, %), but there are many other operators you might use, in a number of categories, including the following:

Operators can be applied to constants, cell references, or functions.

The results of any of these comparisons will be a logical value – either True or False.

The intersection of two ranges is a reference to all the cells that are common between the two ranges.

Operator	Meaning	Examples
Arithmetic		
+ (plus sign)	Addition	**A7+B5**
- (minus sign)	Subtraction Negation	**C6-20** **-C3**
***** (asterisk)	Multiplication	**C5*C6**
/ (forward slash)	Division	**C6/D3**
% (percent sign)	Percent	**20%**
^ (caret)	Exponentiation or Power	**D3^2**
Comparison		
= (equal)	Equal to	**A1=B1**
> (greater than)	Greater than	**A1>B1**
< (less than)	Less than	**A1<B1**
>= (greater than with equal)	Greater than or equal	**A1>=B1**
<= (less than with equal)	Less than or equal	**A1<=B1**
<> (not equal)	Not equal	**A1<>B1**
Text		
& (ampersand)	Connect/join	**"ABCDE"&"FGHI"**
Reference		
: (colon)	Range	**B5:B15**
, (comma)	Union	**SUM(B5:B15,D5:D15)**
(space)	Intersection	**B2:D6 C4:F8**

Calculation Sequence

The order in which a calculation is performed may affect the result. As an example, the calculation **6+4*2** could be interpreted in two different ways. If the addition is performed first, this would give **10*2**, which equals 20. However, if the multiplication is performed first, the calculation becomes **6+8**, which equals 14.

To avoid any ambiguity in calculations, Excel evaluates formulas by applying the operators in a specific order. This is known as "operator precedence". The sequence is as follows:

1	: ,	Colon Space Comma
2	-	Negation
3	%	Percentage
4	^	Exponential
5	* /	Multiplication Division
6	+ -	Addition Subtraction
7	&	Concatenation
8	= < > <= >= <>	Comparison

When the formula has several operators with the same precedence, multiplication and division, for example, Excel evaluates the operators from left to right.

These are some example formulas that illustrate the effect of operator precedence on the calculation result:

You use parentheses to change the order of evaluation, since the expressions within parentheses are evaluated first. If there are parentheses within parentheses, Excel evaluates the expression in the innermost pair of parentheses first, then works outwards.

Functions

Functions are predefined formulas that perform calculations based on specific values, called arguments, provided in the required sequence. The function begins with the function name, followed by an opening parenthesis, the arguments for the function separated by commas, and a closing parenthesis. They are used for many types of calculation, ranging from simple to highly complex.

If you are unsure which function is appropriate for the task, Excel will help you search for the most appropriate. To select a function in the example Invoice worksheet:

Hot tip

Arguments can be numbers, text, cell references, or logical values (True or False).

Don't forget

Several functions in Excel 2019 can be found in the various categories offered on page 88.

Hot tip

To select or change the arguments, click the **Collapse Dialog** button, select the cells on the worksheet, then press the **Expand Dialog** button.

1 Click the cell where you want to use a function as the formula – the total amount cell D6, for example

2 Click **Insert Function**, on the Formula Bar

3 Enter the phrase "add numbers" in the **Search for a function** box, and click **Go** to list related functions

4 Select the appropriate function, in this case **SUM**, and click **OK**

5 Review the arguments suggested – in this case, range D3:D5; see the answer this gives; adjust the range if needed; then click **OK** to **Insert Function**

...cont'd

AutoComplete

Even when you know the function needed, Excel will help you set it up, to help avoid possible syntax and typing errors:

1 Click the worksheet cell, and begin typing the function. For example, click the total cost cell D9 and type **=s**

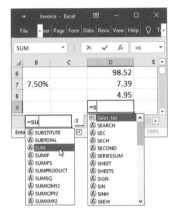

Click on the function name in the prompt, to display help for that function.

2 Excel lists functions that match so far, so you can select a function and see its description, scroll down to see more names, or continue typing – for example, **=su** – to narrow the list

3 When you find the function that you require, double-click the name, then enter the arguments that are shown

4 For example, click D6, press period/full stop, and click D8

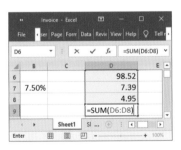

Type the range name, if you have already defined the required cells (see page 63).

5 Type the closing parenthesis, and then press **Enter**

6 The formula with the function is stored in the cell, and the result of the operation will be displayed

As always, you should save the spreadsheet from time-to-time, to preserve your changes.

AutoSum

Select the cell below a
column of numbers

Click **AutoSum**, in the
Editing group on the
Home tab

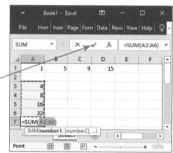

Press **Enter**, or click on the
tick in the Formula Bar, to
add the function

Similarly, select the cell
to the right of a row
of numbers and click
AutoSum to total them

Hot tip

All the cells up or across,
to the first non-numeric
or empty cell, are
included in the total.

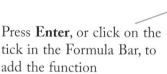

Hot tip

In either case, you can
click the arrow next to
AutoSum, and select
from the list of functions
offered to apply a
different function to the
range of values.

When the selected cell could be
associated with a row or a column,
AutoSum will usually favor the
column. However, you can adjust
the direction or extent of the range
in the formula before you apply it
to the worksheet.

The **AutoSum** function can also be
found in the **Function Library** group,
on the **Formulas** tab, along with **Insert
Function**, **Recently Used,** and various
sets of functions such as **Financial,
Logical,** and **Text**.

Formula Errors

Excel helps you to avoid some of the more common errors when you are entering a formula:

 1 When you type a name, Excel outlines the associated cell or range, so you can confirm that it is the correct selection

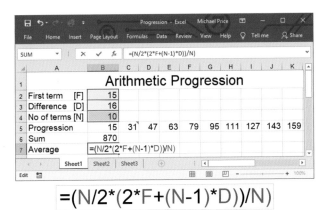

$$=(N/2*(2*F+(N-1)*D))/N)$$

 2 With nested functions, Excel colors the parentheses, to help you ensure that they are in matching open/close pairs

3 If you do make an error, such as the extra parenthesis shown above, it is often detected and corrected

4 If the result overflows the available space, Excel displays **#** hash signs

```
#####
1048576
```

5 There's a similar display for other errors, but, in addition, a green flash shows in the top left-hand corner of the cell

```
#####
#DIV/0!
```

6 Select the cell, then click the information icon for more details and options for dealing with the problem

Hot tip

This totals and averages the terms in a number series, with formulas that have several levels of parentheses. Here, the final parenthesis needs to be deleted, as Excel will detect.

Hot tip

In this example, F, D, and N are defined names.

69

Don't forget

Other common errors displayed this way include **#REF!** (invalid reference) and **#NAME?** (name not recognized).

#REF!
#NAME?

Add Comments

You can add notes to a cell, perhaps to explain the way in which a particular formula operates:

1 Click the cell where the comment is meant to appear

2 Select the **Review** tab, and click **New Comment**, in the **Comments** group

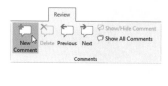

3 Your username is shown, but you can delete this if you prefer, then add your comments

31 | **Michael Price:**
=if(count($B5:B5)<N,B5+D," ")
This formula displays the next number in the series, until the required N terms have been displayed, then it

4 Format text in the comment as desired, and click outside the comment box when you've finished the comment

The presence of a comment is indicated by the red flash at the top-right corner of the cell, and the comment box appears when you move the mouse over the cell

5 The presence of a comment is indicated by the red flash at the top-right corner of the cell, and the comment box appears when you move the mouse over the cell

6 The **Edit Comment** command replaces the **New Comment** command, when the selected cell contains an existing comment

7 Click **Previous** or **Next** to view other comments

5 Excel Tables

The Excel table structure helps you to keep sets of data separate, so that you don't accidentally change other data when you are inserting or deleting rows and columns. There are other benefits also, such as structured cell references, automatic filters, sorts, and subtotals.

72 Create an Excel Table

74 Edit Tables

75 Table Styles

76 Table Totals

77 Count Unique Entries

78 Structured References

79 Calculated Columns

80 Insert Rows

82 Custom Sort

83 Print a Table

84 Summarize a Table

86 Convert to a Range

Create an Excel Table

To make it easier to manage and analyze a group of related data, you can turn a range of cells into an Excel Table. The range should contain no empty rows or empty columns.

To illustrate this feature, a table is used to interpret the genre (music classification) codes contained in the MP3 tags for music files (see pages 40-41). This field often appears as a genre code such as (2) for Country music, or (4) for Disco. Search on the internet for "ID3 genre code table", and select a suitable web page. For example, we found a useful table online at **puszcza.gnu.org. ua/software/idest/manual/html_section/Genre-Codes.html**

Hot tip

In an "Excel Table", the rows and columns are managed independently from the data in other rows and columns on the worksheet. In earlier releases of Excel, this feature was called an "Excel List".

72

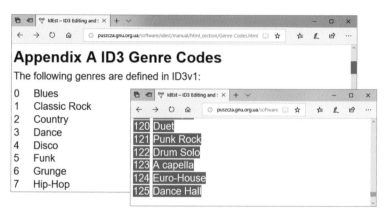

1 Select the table in your web browser, then press **Ctrl + C**

2 Open the "Music List" worksheet, and type headers "GenreID#" and "Genre" in two empty columns

Beware

When Genre is provided as a Genre code in brackets, the value will be treated as a negative number when the data is imported to an Excel worksheet.

(12)

-12

3 Select the second cell in the first of those columns, then press **Ctrl + V** to copy the code table into the worksheet

4 With the data and headers selected, click the **Insert** tab, then click **Table** in the **Tables** group

5 Check that the appropriate range of data is selected

It may be best to remove worksheet protection and unfreeze panes, before you insert the new data.

6 If the first row has headers, select **My table has headers**; otherwise, you'd let Excel generate default headers

◢	A	B	C	G	W	X	Y	Z	AA
1	Track	Title	Artist	Genre	Status		GenreID#	Genre	
2		1 Day Without Rain	Enya	-12	OK			Blues	
3		2 Wild Child	Enya	-12	OK		1	Classic Rock	
4		3 Only Time	Enya	-12	OK		2	Country	
5		4 Tempus Vernum	Enya	-12	OK		3	Dance	
6		5 Deora Ar Mo Chroi	Enya	-12	OK		4	Disco	
7		6 Flora's Secret	Enya	-12	OK		5	Funk	
8		7 Fallen Embers	Enya	-12	OK		6	Grunge	
9		8 Silver Inches	Enya	-12	OK		7	Hip-Hop	
10		9 Pilgrim	Enya	-12	OK		8	Jazz	

If you click in the table, the context-sensitive **Table Tools Design** tab is displayed, so that you can customize or edit the table settings.

The table is given the default banding style, and **Filter** buttons are automatically added in the header row of each column, allowing you to sort or filter the contents. The table will be given a default name, such as "Table1". To change this name:

1 Click in the table, and click the **Design** tab

2 Click the **Table Name** box in the **Properties** group, to highlight the name

3 Type a new name for the table – e.g. "Code" – and press **Enter** to apply the change (and update all references to the old table name)

You can also change the names of tables, using the **Name Manager** on the **Formulas** tab (see page 63).

Edit Tables

 1 Select the music data and click **Table** on the **Insert** tab, to create another table, and change its name to "Music"

You can insert more than one table in the same worksheet, and work with each of them independently. Inserting or deleting rows or columns in one table will not affect other tables.

Click adjacent cells to delete more than one column or row in the table at a time.

74

 2 Click any unrequired columns in the new "Music" table, then select **Home**, click the arrow next to **Delete** in the **Cells** group, and choose **Delete Table Columns**

 3 Click in the last cell of the "Code" table, and press **Tab** – to add a row

4 Type an entry, such as "143", "Salsa", then add a row with "146", "Jpop" and a row with "255", "Unknown"

Don't click the **Delete** button itself, or you will delete the cells rather than display the menu. If you do delete cells, go to the Quick Access Toolbar and press the **Undo** button.

 5 Select the cells with values 143 and 146, then select the **Home** tab, and choose **Cells**, **Delete**, **Delete Table Rows**

Table Styles

The **Design** tab provides options to change the formatting of the rows and columns in the table.

 1 Specify if there's a header row, and turn banding on or off, using settings in the **Table Style Options** group

Styles are grouped into light, medium, and dark sets, with additional effects for end columns, and for banding.

2 Click the **Quick Styles** button, in the **Table Styles** group, to view the full list of styles

3 The Styles selection bar is displayed, if there's room on the Ribbon, and you can scroll the styles, or press the **More** button to show the full list

4 Move the mouse pointer over a style option, and the table will illustrate the effects that would apply

Any changes you make to the **Table Style Options** will be remembered and selected the next time you review the settings.

Table Totals

You can add a Total Row at the end of the table, and display the totals for columns (or use another function appropriate to the type of information stored in the column).

To add table totals:

 Click in the table, select the **Design** tab, and click the **Total Row** box in the **Table Style Options** group

2 The Total row is added as the last row of the table, and the last column is assigned a value – in this example, Bitrate is shown with a total value of 478

3 Select the Total cell, and click the arrow to see the function applied – in this case, the function is **103 - Counta**, which counts non-blank cells in the column

4 You can apply a total to any column. For Title, Comment and FilePath you could use **Counta** again

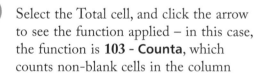

5 For Length you'd perhaps use **Sum**; and for Year, **Min**

Count Unique Entries

For the Artist column, you can count all unique entries, to give the numbers of individual artists stored in the table:

1 Click in the Total cell for the Artist column, and begin typing the function **=sum(1/countif(**

2 Click the Artist header, to extend the formula

3 Type a comma, click the Artist header again, and then type two closing parentheses

4 This is an array formula, so press **Shift + Ctrl + Enter** (rather than just **Enter**), and the count will be displayed

Hot tip

This calculates the frequency for each entry, inverts these counts, and sums up the resulting fractions. For example, if an entry appears three times, you get 1/3 + 1/3 + 1/3 for that entry, giving a count of 1. Each unique entry adds another 1.

Beware

This method of counting the number of duplicate entries assumes there are no empty cells in the range being checked.

Don't forget

Use a similar formula to count the number of unique entries in the Album column.

{=SUM(1/COUNTIF([Album],[Album]))}		
Artist	Album	Year
Hayley Westenra	Winter Magic	2009
Hayley Westenra	Winter Magic	2009
18	40	1975

Structured References

The formulas shown for the totals illustrate the use of structured references. These allow you to refer to the contents of a table, using meaningful names, without having to be concerned about the specific row numbers and column letters, or changes that are caused when rows and columns are added or deleted. The structured references use the table name and column specifiers:

=Music	All data in a table named "Music".
=Music[Length]	All data in a Music table's column named "Length".

You can add a special item specifier to refer to particular parts:

=Music[#All]	The entire Music table, including headers, data and totals.
=Music[#Data]	All data in a Music table.
=Music[#Headers]	The header row of a Music table.
=Music[#Totals]	The totals row of a Music table.
=[@Length]	The intersection of the "Length" column with the active row (n).

Formulas within the table, such as subtotals on the Totals row, can leave off the table name. This forms an unqualified structured reference; e.g. **[Filename]**. However, outside the table, you need the fully qualified structured reference; e.g. **Music[Filename]**.

This formula includes two subtotal functions (see page 76) to obtain the minimum and the maximum values from the Bitrate column. The results are separated by a hyphen, and the three items are concatenated (joined), to form a single text string. This is displayed in the cell K482, which contains the formula.

Calculated Columns

You can add a calculated column to an Excel table. This uses a single formula that adjusts for each row, automatically expanding to include additional rows.

Start by inserting a new column in the table:

1 Click the far right column of a table, then select the **Home** tab, and click the arrow next to **Insert** – which is found in the **Cells** group

2 Click **Insert Table Columns to the Right**, and then rename the new column as "Style" (i.e. style of music)

You need to enter the formula only once, and you won't need to use the **Fill** or **Copy** command when the table grows.

(Excel screenshot showing formula bar: =vlookup(-[@Genre],Code,2,false))

	F	G	H	I	J	K	L	M	N	O
1	Length	Genre	Commen	FilePath	FileSize	Bitrate	Style		GenreID#	Genre
2	0:02:37	-12		C:\Users\M	3,795,536	192			0	Blues
3	0:03:47	-12		C:\Users\M	5,465,704	192			1	Classic Rock
4	0:03:37	-12		C:\Users\M	5,228,450	192	re],Code,2,false)			Country
5	0:02:24	-12		C:\Users\M	3,460,626	192			3	Dance
6	0:02:48	-12		C:\Users\M	4,052,822	192			4	Disco

3 Click anywhere in the Style column and type a formula – e.g. **=VLOOKUP(1[@Genre],Code,2,FALSE)** – then press **Enter** to update the cells in the column

(Excel screenshot showing formula bar: =VLOOKUP(-[@Genre],Code,2,FALSE))

	F	G	H	I	J	K	L	M	N	O
1	Length	Genre	Commen	FilePath	FileSize	Bitrate	Style		GenreID#	Genre
2	0:02:37	-12		C:\Users\M	3,795,536	192	Other		0	Blues
3	0:03:47	-12		C:\Users\M	5,465,704	192	Other		1	Classic Rock
4	0:03:37	-12		C:\Users\M	5,228,450	192	Other		2	Country
5	0:02:24	-12		C:\Users\M	3,460,626	192	Other		3	Dance
6	0:02:48	-12		C:\Users\M	4,052,822	192	Other		4	Disco

The **VLOOKUP** formula in this example is a vertical table lookup. It matches the value 1, in the first column of the Code table (the GenreID#). It then copies the associated value on that row in the second column of the code table (the Genre) into the Styles column. See page 90 for an example of an **HLOOKUP** (a horizontal lookup).

4 The formula is automatically filled in to all the cells in the column, above as well as below the active cell

Insert Rows

1 Scroll to the last cell in the table, press **Tab** to add a new row, and you'll see that the new formula is replicated

Beware

Adding empty rows may cause temporary errors in formulas that need data in all cells, as illustrated here. The problems will be resolved as soon as the data gets added.

2 To add data from a text file (see pages 42-43), click a cell in an empty part of the worksheet and select **From Text/CSV** (on the **Data** tab in the **Get & Transform Data** group)

3 Locate and double-click the data file, then use the **Text Import Wizard** to specify the structure of the data file

Hot tip

You cannot import data directly from an external source into the table, so you must use another part of the worksheet as an interim.

4 Select **Load, Load To...** and choose **Table, Existing worksheet** to add the data to the temporary location

5 Click **OK** to load the data into the worksheet

6 Highlight the new data (excluding the header row), select the **Home** tab, and click **Copy** from the **Clipboard** group

7 Select the first cell in the new row added to the table then click **Paste**, from the **Clipboard** group

8 Additional rows are put into the table as necessary, to hold the new data records

Microsoft Excel

This table inserted rows into your worksheet. This may cause data in cells below the table to shift down.

☐ Do not display this dialog again

OK

9 The data records are copied into the new rows in the extended table

10 You'll see that totals are updated and Style, the calculated column, displays the associated values for the new entries

Custom Sort

When new rows are inserted, it may be appropriate to sort the table, to position the new rows where they belong.

To do this:

 Click in the table, select the **Home** tab, click **Sort & Filter** in the **Editing** group, and select **Custom Sort...**

Or

Click in the table, select the **Data** tab, and click **Sort**, in the **Sort & Filter** group

B	C
Title ▼	Artist ⬆

2 The first time there are no criteria defined, so click the arrow in **Sort by** to add a header (e.g. Artist)

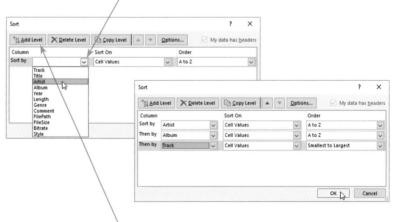

 Click the **Add Level** button and choose a second header (e.g. Album), then add a third level (e.g. Track) and then click **OK** to apply the sort sequence

Print a Table

You can print a table without having to select the print area specifically (see pages 32-33):

1 Click any of its cells to select the table

2 Use **Filters** to restrict the data to print; e.g. a specific artist

3 Press the **File** tab, then select **Print** (or press **Ctrl + P**)

4 For **Settings**, choose **Print Selected Table**, then adjust the paper size and scaling, if needed

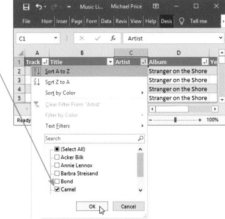

5 Specify the number of copies required, then click the **Print** button to complete the process

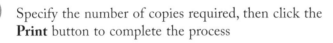

You may wish to change to a different table style; one more suitable for printing (or select **None** for a plain effect).

Table Styles

Some formulas on a Total Row, if present, may continue to reference the whole of the table contents.

You can print the active worksheet, the entire workbook, the selected data, or the active table.

	Print Active Sheets
	Only print the active sheets
	Print Entire Workbook
	Print the entire workbook
	Print Selection
	Only print the current selection
	Print Selected Table
	Only print the selected table
	Ignore Print Area

Summarize a Table

You can summarize the data, using the **PivotTable** feature. See page 165 for another example.

Select **Insert** and click **Recommended PivotTables** to see the suggestions that Excel 2019 makes for the data in your worksheets.

Click the **Collapse Dialog** box, select the first cell of the location, then click the **Expand Dialog** box to add the report to the worksheet.

1 Click in the table, select the **Insert** tab, and then click the **PivotTable** button, in the **Tables** group

2 Choose the location for the **PivotTable** report, either a new worksheet or an empty portion of the current worksheet, and then click **OK**

3 An empty **PivotTable** report is added at the specified location

4 Check the boxes to select fields from the list (for example, Track, Artist, Album, and Length)

By default, text fields are added to the **Row Labels** area, and fields containing numbers are added to the **Values** area.

5 Rearrange the fields by dragging between areas, or right-click a name and select the area where it should appear. For example, move the Length field to the **Values** area

6 Click a numeric field in the **Values** list to reposition, move to a different area, or change **Value Field Settings**

7 Choose how you wish to summarize the values (Sum, Count, Average, Min, Max; etc.)

8 Choose a **Custom Name** for the field, then click **OK** to see the PivotTable report

When you click a field name that has text values, and then select **Field Settings**, it will display appropriate text options for that field.

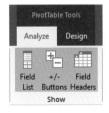

Analyze and Design tabs are added to the Ribbon. Select **Field List** in the **Analyze**, **Show** group to hide or reveal the **PivotTable Fields** list. From here, you can also collapse or expand the report details.

Convert to a Range

You can turn an Excel table back into a range of data:

1 Click in the table, then select the **Design** tab and click **Convert to Range** in the **Tools** group

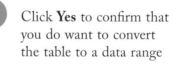

If you have just created a table from a range of data (see pages 72-73), you can switch back to the range form by clicking **Undo** on the Quick Access Toolbar.

2 Click **Yes** to confirm that you do want to convert the table to a data range

3 The cell styles will be preserved, but the filter boxes will be removed from the headers

4 The Total row will still appear, but all references will now be standard **$A$1**-style absolute cell references

5 To convert the range back into the table, you will need to recreate formulas for the Totals row and calculated columns

To remove the table style from the cells, select all the data, click the **Home** tab, click the Down arrow next to **Cell Styles** in the **Styles** group, and choose the **Normal** style.

6 Advanced Functions

There is a large library of Excel functions available. To help locate the ones you want, related functions are grouped by category, and there's a Recently Used list. More functions are provided via Excel Add-ins. With nested functions in your formulas, use the Evaluate command to see how they work.

88 Function Library

89 Logical Functions

90 Lookup/Reference Functions

92 Financial Functions

94 Date & Time Functions

96 Text Functions

98 Math & Trig Functions

100 Random Numbers

101 Statistical Functions

102 Engineering Functions

103 Excel Add-ins

104 Evaluate Formula

Function Library

Don't forget

Select **More Functions** for other categories including **Statistical**, **Engineering** and **Web**.

Hot tip

The **Function Library** continues to expand with each version of Excel, from a total of 320 in Excel 2007 to around some 460 functions in Excel 2019.

 Select the **Formulas** tab to see the **Function Library** group, with a Ribbon style that depends on your current window size

The **Insert Function** command, on the left of the group, will allow you to enter keywords to search for a function (see page 66). It provides the syntax and a brief description for any function that you select, plus a link to more detailed help. Alternatively, you can select from one of the categories.

 Click any of the category entries for an alphabetical list of the names of the functions that it includes. The categories, and the number of functions included in each, are:

Most Recently Used	10	**Text**	28
All	459	**Logical**	11
Financial	55	**Information**	20
Date & Time	24	**Engineering**	54
Math & Trig	74	**Cube**	7
Statistical	110	**Compatibility**	42
Lookup & Reference	19	**Web**	3
Database	12		

All

All provides an alphabetical list from ABS to ZTEST of every function included in Excel, giving you a way to search for a function when you have no idea which category it belongs to.

Most Recently Used

Most Recently Used remembers the functions you last used, allowing you to make repeated use of functions with the minimum of fuss, without needing their particular categories.

Logical Functions

Sometimes the value for one cell depends on the value in another cell. For example, test scores could be used to set grade levels.

1 The formula in C2 is **=B2>=50** and gives the result True or False, depending on the value that is in B2

Comparisons (e.g. using the **<, =,** or **>** operators) that are either True or False are the basis of logical functions.

2 To display the more meaningful results of Pass or Fail, you can use an **IF** formula, such as that shown in cell D2: **=IF(B2>=50,"Pass","Fail")**

The **AND** function includes a set of logical tests, all of which must be True, to give a True result.

3 Sometimes you need to check two conditions; e.g. in E3 the formula **=IF(AND(B3>=50,B4>=50),"Merit","n/a")**

The **IF** functions can be nested, with the False value being replaced by another **IF** function, to make a further test. For example, this formula gives the country code, if the name matches, or goes on to test for the next country name in the list.

You could use an **OR** function for the first two countries here, since a match for either would give the same code.

Lookup/Reference Functions

If you have a number of items to check against, set up a list. Here is an example using country codes:

 This worksheet has a list of country names (in alphabetic order) with their dialing codes, stored in range D1:IF2

You can have up to 64 levels of nesting, but long **IF** formulas can be awkward to type in. A better alternative may be a **lookup** function.

This range is named "IDC" (International Dialing Code)

 Type "=hlookup(" in cell B2 for the lookup function

For the "range_lookup" argument, you specify a logical value of **TRUE**, to get close matches, or **FALSE**, to allow exact matches only.

 This requires a value ("USA"), the lookup range ("IDC"), the results row (2), and a logical Match value

Copy the formula downwards, to look up the codes for the other countries

A mistype of "Andorra" gives the result **#N/A** – no match found.

...cont'd

To reverse the process, and replace a number with a text value, you could use the **CHOOSE** function. For example:

 To convert the value of cell B2 into a rank, enter in B3
=CHOOSE(B2,"First","Second","Third","Fourth","Fifth")
– then copy the formula across to Rank cells C3 to F3

Hot tip

The contents of B2 are used as an index, to select from the list of 5 values provided. A maximum of 254 values could be used.

	A	B	C	D	E	F	G	H	I
1		Tom	Dick	Harry	Yvonne	Khan			
2	Position	3	5	2	1	4			
3	Rank	Third	Fifth	Second	First	Fourth			

B3 formula: =CHOOSE(B2,"First","Second","Third","Fourth","Fifth")

 To apply a suffix to the position value, enter in B4 the formula **=B2&CHOOSE(B2,"st","nd","rd","th","th")** – then copy the formula across to Standing cells C4 to F4

Hot tip

Here, the suffix chosen from the list is appended to the index number.

91

	A	B	C	D	E	F	G	H	I
1		Tom	Dick	Harry	Yvonne	Khan			
2	Position	3	5	2	1	4			
3	Rank	Third	Fifth	Second	First	Fourth			
4	Standing	3rd	5th	2nd	1st	4th			

B4 formula: =B2&CHOOSE(B2,"st","nd","rd","th","th")

 You could store the values in a range of cells, but you must list the relevant cells individually in the formula

Beware

Index values outside the range provided (in these examples, 1-5) will cause a **#VALUE!** error.

	A	B	C	D	E	F	G	H	I
1		Tom	Dick	Harry	Yvonne	Khan		Top	
2	Position	3	5	2	1	4		Runner Up	
3	Rank	Third	Fifth	Second	First	Fourth		Also Ran	
4	Standing	3rd	5th	2nd	1st	4th		Finished	
5								Finished	
6	Status	Also Ran	Finished	Runner Up	Top	Finished			

B6 formula: =CHOOSE(B2,$H$1,$H$2,$H$3,$H$4,$H$5)

You should use absolute cell references for the values, so you can copy the formula without having to adjust the references.

Financial Functions

Excel includes specialized functions for dealing with investments, securities, loans, and other financial transactions. For example, to calculate the monthly payments required for a mortgage, you'd use the **PMT** function.

To illustrate, assume a purchase price of $250,000, interest at 6% per annum, and a 30-year period:

 Enter the initial information into a worksheet, then, for the payment, begin typing the function **=PMT(**

 Click the **Insert Function** button, to display the input form for the function arguments

3 For the **Rate**, put the interest rate per payment period **B2/D2** (6%/12). For **Nper** (number of payments) put **C2*D2** (30*12), and for **PV** (present value) put A2 ($250,000)

 Click **OK** to show the payment per month on the worksheet

...cont'd

Perhaps you'd like to know what would happen if you paid the mortgage off over a shorter period:

 1 Select the existing values and calculation, then drag down, using the Fill Handle, to replicate into three more rows

	A	B	C	D	E
1	Purchase Price	Interest Rate	Duration	Payments/Year	Payment
2	250000	6.00%	30	12	($1,498.88)
3	250000	6.00%	25	12	($1,610.75)
4	250000	6.00%	20	12	($1,791.08)
5	250000	6.00%	15	12	($2,109.64)

E5 =PMT(B5/D5,C5*D5,A5)

You could type a new value into the Duration cell and see the new payment. However, copying the rows makes it easier to compare the different options.

2 Change the duration to 25, 20 and 15 years, on successive rows, and observe the revised monthly payments required

3 Add a column for total interest paid, then enter the cumulative interest function **=CUMIPMT(** and click the **Insert Function** button once more

F2 =CUMIPMT(B2/D2,C2*D2,A2,1,C2*D2,0)

	A	B	C	D	E	F
1	Purchase Price	Interest Rate	Duration	Payments/Year	Payment	Total Interest
2	250000	6.00%	30	12	($1,498.88)	C2*D2,0)
3	250000	6.00%	25			
4	250000	6.00%	20			
5	250000	6.00%	15			

Function Arguments

CUMIPMT

Rate	B2/D2	= 0.005
Nper	C2*D2	= 360
Pv	A2	= 250000
Start_period	1	= 1
End_period	C2*D2	= 360

= -289595.4726

Returns the cumulative interest paid between two periods.

    Rate is the interest rate.

Formula result = ($289,595.47)

Help on this function

The **CUMIPMT** function arguments are similar to those for **PMT**, with "Type" now mandatory (set it to 0, for payment at end of month).

You can calculate the interest over any part of the loan, but putting the first and last payments gives the total interest over the whole period of the loan.

4 Copy the formula down, to see the cumulative interest for all the loan durations

F5 =CUMIPMT(B5/

	C	D	E	F
1	Duration	Payments/Year	Payment	Total Interest
2	30	12	($1,498.88)	($289,595.47)
3	25	12	($1,610.75)	($233,226.05)
4	20	12	($1,791.08)	($179,858.64)
5	15	12	($2,109.64)	($129,735.57)

Date & Time Functions

Date and time values (see page 59) are stored as numbers, and count the days since the starting point (usually January 1st, 1900). However, they can be displayed in various date or time formats.

Hot tip

Excel also supports the 1904 date system, the default for Apple Mac computers, where a date value of 1 is taken as January 2nd, 1904.

 The whole-number portion of the value converts into month, day, and year (with account taken for leap years), so 45651 represents December 25, 2024

	A	B	C	D	E
1	Value	Date	Date and Time	Time	
2	43584.1234	April 29, 2019	4/29/19 2:57 AM	2:57:42 AM	2:57:42
3	45651.6789	December 25, 2024	12/25/24 4:17 PM	4:17:37 PM	16:17:37

Beware

You can use date and time values in formulas, but, because of the calendar effects, the results may not always be what you'd expect.

 The decimal portion of the value indicates the time of day, so .1234 is 2:57AM, and .6789 is 4:17PM (or 16:17 if you've specified the 24-hour clock)

	A	B
1	Value	Date
2	43584.1234	April 29, 2019
3	45651.6789	December 25, 2024
4	Difference	2067.56
5	Days	-4.00
6	Months	8.00
7	Years	5.00
8	Total Months	68.00
9	Ten Days	January 4, 2025
10		January 8, 2025

	A	B
1	Value	Date
2	43584.1234	=A2
3	45651.6789	=A3
4	Difference	=A3-A2
5	Days	=DAY(A3)-DAY(A2)
6	Months	=MONTH(A3)-MONTH(A2)
7	Years	=YEAR(A3)-YEAR(A2)
8	Total Months	=(YEAR(A3)-YEAR(A2))*12+MONTH(A3)-MONTH(A2)
9	Ten Days	=A3+10
10		=WORKDAY(A3,10)

Don't forget

In the example, the value of the date is displayed to illustrate the options. You type the date – e.g. as 6/14/2019 – and Excel automatically converts it into a number value, and then stores it in the cell. The cell format controls what's displayed.

B4	Difference in days
B5	Subtracts calendar day numbers (may be minus)
B6	Subtracts calendar months (may be minus)
B7	Difference in years (ignores the part year)
B8	Twelve months for every year +/- the difference in months
B9	Adding ten calendar days to A3 gives Jan 4, 2014
B10	Adding ten work days (to allow for weekends and holidays) gives the later date Jan 8, 2014

There's a worksheet function **DATEDIF** that's not listed in the **Date & Time** category (though it is described in Excel **Help**):

=DATEDIF(StartDate, EndDate, Interval)

The interval code controls the result that the function produces:

Interval value	Calculates the number between the dates of
"y"	Whole years
"m"	Whole months
"d"	Days in total
"ym"	Whole months, ignoring the years
"yd"	Days, ignoring the years
"md"	Days, ignoring the months and years

Hot tip

Excel's Visual Basic for Applications (VBA) has a similar function called **DateDiff**, but without the **"ym"**, **"yd"**, and **"md"** interval parameters.

When entering the interval code into **DATEDIF** as a constant, you enclose it in quotes. However, if your interval code is stored in a worksheet cell, it should not be enclosed in quotes in the cell.

1 Use the **DATEDIF** function with each of these codes in turn, to calculate the difference between the dates that are stored in cells B2 and B3

2 This function is useful when calculating someone's exact age, in years, months, and days. For example, **DATEDIF** applied to a date of birth and a more current date gives:

Hot tip

DATEDIF is applied three times, to obtain the years, months, and days, and the results are joined together into a single statement.

The **&** operators concatenate the results of the calculations, with literal text values for years, months, and days.

Text Functions

Values can be presented in many different ways, even though they remain stored as numbers. Sometimes, however, you actually want to convert the values into text (enclosed in quotes), perhaps to include them in a specific format, in a report or message. To do this you would use the **TEXT** function. Its syntax is:

=TEXT(value, format)

Don't forget

The **DOLLAR** function will display the value in the default currency format for your system; for example, using the Pound Sterling symbol (£) for UK systems.

1 Format a number as text, with a fixed number of decimal places, and with a comma as the thousands separator, if desired

2 Display a number in money format, using any currency symbol

3 Display a number using the default currency for your system

	A	B
1	Value	1234.5678
2		
3	"=TEXT(B1,"0.00")	1234.57
4	"=TEXT(B1,"#,##0.00")	1,234.57
5		
6		
7	"=TEXT(B1,"€0.00")	€1234.57
8		
9		
10	"DOLLAR(B1,2)	$1,234.57
11		
12		
13	"=TEXT(DATE(2019,4,29),"dddd")	Monday
14	"=TEXT(DATE(2019,12,25),"ddd")	Wed

4 Show the day of the week, for a date value, using the long or short form of the day name

Hot tip

You can use any of the number formats shown in the **Format Cells** dialog (see page 58), other than **General** format.

5 For examples of the number formats, choose the **Custom** category in the **Format Cells** dialog, and scroll the list

Format Cells dialog with Custom category selected, showing number format type codes.

There are several functions provided to help you manipulate a piece of text, to make it more suitable for presentation:

1 Remove all extraneous blanks, leaving a single space between words

2 Convert all the characters in the text into lowercase format

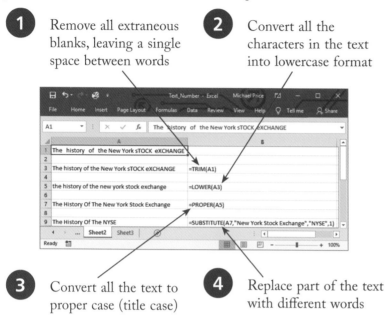

3 Convert all the text to proper case (title case)

4 Replace part of the text with different words

Excel does not have an explicit Word Count function, but the text functions can be used in combination, to find the number of words that are in a cell.

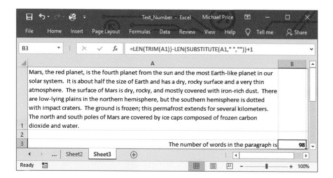

The **TRIM** function removes multiple spaces from the text, then the first **LEN** function counts all the characters, including spaces. The **SUBSTITUTE** function removes all spaces from the text, then the second **LEN** function counts the remaining characters. The difference between the two lengths is the number of spaces between words. Add one to find the number of words in the cell.

Hot tip

These functions don't change the text in cell A1. Only the working copies used during the calculation are modified.

Don't forget

The **SUBSTITUTE** function replaces every instance of the text specified, unless you indicate the specific occurrence that you want to change.

Hot tip

The text functions can help you tidy up text data you import from an external source – especially if you repeat the import on a regular basis to update the data.

Math & Trig Functions

These functions allow you to carry out calculations using cell contents, computed values, and constants. For example:

1 The **PRODUCT** function multiplies price times (1 - discount) quantity to get the cost of the item

2 Copy the formula, to calculate the costs for the other items

3 The total cost is the sum of the costs for all the individual items

You may sometimes want to make calculations without showing all of the intermediate values. For example:

1 The total cost (before discount) is the sum of the products of the item prices and item quantities; i.e. **B3*D3 + B4*D4 + ...**

2 This value is calculated with the **SUMPRODUCT** function, which multiplies the sets of cells and totals the results

3 Rather than using the **SUMPRODUCT** function to calculate the total discount, you can simply subtract actual cost from total cost.

This avoids problems with rounding errors, which can show up in even straightforward functions, such as **SUM**

...cont'd

To illustrate the type of problem that can arise, imagine placing an order for goods where there's a special gift offered for spending $140 or more.

1 A quick check seems to indicate that the total is just over the amount required

	A	B	C	D	E	F
1			Sales Invoice			
2	Item	Price	Discount	Quantity	Cost	
3	DVD	49.99	1/3	1	33.33	
4	CD	19.99	1/3	1	13.33	
5	Book	16.99	1/3	1	11.33	140.01
6	Pad	1.39	1/3	10	9.27	
7	Flash	13.99	1/3	7	65.29	
8	Gizmo	11.19	1/3	1	7.46	
9	TOTAL				139.99	
10		Spend $140 to get that Special Gift				
11						
12	Total Cost				209.99	
13	Total discount				70.00	

E9 formula: =SUM(E3:E8)

2 But the total that Excel calculates appears to be just under that amount

Excel hasn't got its sums wrong – the stored numbers that it totals aren't quite the same as those on display.

3 Change the cell format, to show more decimal places, and you'll see the actual values are slightly lower than those initially shown

33.326667
13.326667
11.326667
9.266667
65.286667
7.460000
139.993333

4 Click cell E3, and add the **ROUND** function – to round the item cost to two places

E3 formula: =ROUND(B3*(1-C3)*D3,2)

	A	B	C	D	E
1			Sales Invoice		
2	Item	Price	Discount	Quantity	Cost
3	DVD	49.99	1/3	1	33.33
4	CD	19.99	1/3	1	13.33
5	Book	16.99	1/3	1	11.33
6	Pad	1.39	1/3	10	9.27
7	Flash	13.99	1/3	7	65.29
8	Gizmo	11.19	1/3	1	7.46
9	TOTAL				140.01
10		Special Gift Enclosed			
12	Total Cost				209.99
13	Total discount				69.98

5 Copy the new formula into cells E4:E8 to see the expected amount

The **ROUND** function rounds up or down. So, 1.234 becomes 1.23, while 1.236 becomes 1.24 (rounded to two decimal places). You can specify a negative number of places, to round the values to the nearest multiple of ten (-1 places) or of one hundred (-2 places); and so on.

33.330000
13.330000
11.330000
9.270000
65.290000
7.460000
140.010000

Hot tip

Values may be displayed, or converted to text, with a fixed number of decimal digits, but the original value will still have the same number of digits as originally typed, or as calculated when the value was created.

Beware

You will find that what you see on the worksheet isn't always what you get in the calculations.

66

Don't forget

In some cases, you may always want to round the values in the same direction. Excel provides the functions **ROUNDUP** and **ROUNDDOWN** for those situations.

Random Numbers

It is sometimes useful to produce sets of random numbers. This could be for sample data, when creating or testing worksheets. Another use might be to select a variety of tracks from your music library, to generate a playlist.

Hot tip

RAND generates a number from 0 to 1. **=RAND()*99+101** would give numbers between 101 and 200. Unlike those produced by the **RANDBETWEEN** function, these aren't whole numbers.

1 Click A1 and enter the function **=RAND()**, to provide a random number between 0 and 1

2 Copy A1 down through A2:A5 and a different number will be shown in each cell

3 Click C1 and enter the function **=RANDBETWEEN(1,10)** to generate a whole number less than or equal to 10

4 Copy C1 down through C2:C5 to provide numbers for each cell, with possible repeats since there are only ten possibilities

Hot tip

To generate a random number that doesn't change each time the worksheet is recalculated, type **=RAND()** on the Formula Bar, and then press **F9**. The generated number is placed into the cell as a literal value.

5 You can generate negative random numbers. For example, cells E1:E5 have values between -99 and +99

6 Select the **Formulas** tab, click **Calculate Now** in the **Calculation** group, and the numbers will be regenerated

Statistical Functions

There's a large number of statistical functions, but the most likely one to be used is the **AVERAGE** function.

1 Create a block A1:E5 of random numbers between 101 and 200, to use as data for the functions

	A	B	C	D	E
1	183	110	164	178	152
2	122	167	165	159	159
3	176	197	177	132	180
4	144	191	126	119	195
5	133	185	185	139	110

A1 =RANDBETWEEN(101,200)

2 Define "Sample" as the name for the range **$A$1:$A$5**

3 Select and copy A1:E5, then select the **Home** tab, click the arrow on the **Paste** command, and select **Paste Values** (to replace the formula with the literal value, in each cell)

Hot tip

Using **Copy**, **Paste**, then **Paste Values**, to replace the formulas with their values, means that the set of random numbers generated won't later be affected by recalculation of the worksheet.

Calculate typical statistics:

1 The arithmetic mean is **=AVERAGE(Sample)**

2 The number in the middle of the sample is **=MEDIAN(Sample)**

	A	B	C	D	E
1	183	110	164	178	152
2	122	167	165	159	159
3	176	197	177	132	180
4	144	191	126	119	195
5	133	185	185	139	110
6					
7		=AVERAGE(Sample)			157.92
8		=MEDIAN(Sample)			164
9		=MODE(Sample)			110
10		=COUNT(Sample)			25
11		=COUNTIF(Sample,">=150")			16
12		=MAX(Sample)			197
13		=MIN(Sample)			110

A1 183

3 The most frequently occurring value is **=MODE(Sample)**

4 The number of values in the sample is **=COUNT(Sample)**

5 The number of values in the sample that are greater than or equal to 150 is **=COUNTIF(Sample,">=150")**

6 The maximum value in the sample is **=MAX(Sample)**

7 The minimum value in the sample is **=MIN(Sample)**

Don't forget

There are a number of different ways to interpret the term "average". Make sure that you use the function that's appropriate for your requirements.

Engineering Functions

There are some rather esoteric functions in the **Engineering** category, but some are quite generally applicable; for example:

 Convert from one measurement system to another, using the function **=CONVERT(value, from_unit, to_unit)**

A5			f_x	=CONVERT(CONVERT(1,"m","ft"),"m","ft")		
	A	B	C		D	E
1	0.832674185		=CONVERT(1,"pt","uk_pt")		Convert 1 US pint to UK pints	
2	82.4		=CONVERT(28,"C","F")		Convert 28°C to °F	
3	3600		=CONVERT(1,"pt","uk_pt")		Convert 1 hour to seconds	
4	0.868976242		=CONVERT(1,"lbm","g")		Convert 1 pound to grams	
5	10.76391042		=CONVERT(CONVERT(1,"m","ft"),"m","ft")		Convert 1 square meter to square feet	

This function deals with units of weight and mass; distance; time; pressure; force; energy; power; magnetism; temperature; and liquids. There are functions to convert between any two pairs of number systems, including binary, decimal, hexadecimal, and octal.

 Convert decimal values to their binary, octal, and hexadecimal equivalents

C18			f_x	=DEC2BIN(A18)		
	A	B	C	D	E	F
1	Decimal		Binary	Octal	Hexadecimal	Roman
2	0		=DEC2BIN(A2)	=DEC2OCT(A2)	=DEC2HEX(A2)	=ROMAN(A2)
3	1		1	1	1	I
4	2		10	2	2	II
5	3		11	3	3	III
6	4		100	4	4	IV
7	5		101	5	5	V
8	6		110	6	6	VI
9	7		111	7	7	VII
10	8		1000	10	8	VIII
11	9		1001	11	9	IX
12	10		1010	12	A	X
13	11		1011	13	B	XI
14	12		1100	14	C	XII
15	13		1101	15	D	XIII
16	14		1110	16	E	XIV
17	15		1111	17	F	XV
18	16		10000	20	10	XVI

There's a **ROMAN** function, which converts Arabic numerals to Roman numerals, but it comes from **Math & Trig** category, which also has the **ARABIC** function for the reverse process.

=ROMAN(1499,0)	MCDXCIX
=ROMAN(1499,1)	MLDVLIV
=ROMAN(1499,2)	MXDIX
=ROMAN(1499,3)	MVDIV
=ROMAN(1499,4)	MID

Excel Add-ins

There are **Add-ins** included with Excel, but they must be loaded before they can be used:

1 Click the **File** tab, and then click the **Options** button

2 Click the **Add-ins** category and, in the **Manage** box, select **Excel Add-ins** and then click **Go**

Excel Options	? ×
General	View and manage Microsoft Office Add-ins.
Formulas	
Data	**Add-ins**
Proofing	
Save	Name ▲ / Location / Type
Language	**Active Application Add-ins**
Ease of Access	*No Active Application Add-ins*
Advanced	
Customize Ribbon	**Inactive Application Add-ins**
Quick Access Toolbar	Analysis ToolPak C:\...Office16\Library\Analysis\ANALYS32.XLL Excel Add-in
Add-ins	Analysis ToolPak - VBA C:\...ice16\Library\Analysis\ATPVBAEN.XLAM Excel Add-in
Trust Center	Date (XML) C:\...\Microsoft Shared\Smart Tag\MOFL.DLL Action
	Euro Currency Tools C:\...\root\Office16\Library\EUROTOOL.XLAM Excel Add-in

Add-in: Euro Currency Tools
Publisher:
Compatibility: No compatibility information available
Location: C:\Program Files (x86)\Microsoft Office\root\Office16\Library\EUROTOOL.XLAM

Description: Conversion and formatting for the euro currency

Manage: Excel Add-ins ▼ [Go...]

[OK] [Cancel]

3 To load the Excel **Add-in**, select the associated check box, and then click **OK**

4 You may be prompted to install some of the add-in programs that you select

5 The new functions that have been added can be found on the **Formulas** tab in the **Solutions** group, or on the **Data** tab in the **Analyze** group

Evaluate Formula

If you are not sure exactly how a formula works, especially when there are nested functions, use the **Evaluate** command to run the formula one step at a time. To use this:

 Select the cell with the formula you wish to investigate

This is the formula for rounding the item costs, as shown in Step 4 on page 99.

Select the **Formulas** tab, click the **Formula Auditing** button, and then select the **Evaluate Formula** command

Press the **Step In** button, to check details like the value of a constant, or to see the expansion of range or table names.

Click **Step Out** to carry on with the evaluation.

Click **Restart**, or else click **Close** when you reach the end.

 Press **Evaluate** repeatedly, to run the calculation forwards, a step at a time

 The expressions in the formula are calculated in turn

ROUND(B3*(1-C3)*D3,2)

ROUND(49.99*(1-C3)*D3,2)

ROUND(49.99*(1-0.333333333333333)*D3,2)

ROUND(49.99*(0.666666666666667)*D3,2)

ROUND(49.99*0.666666666666667*D3,2)

ROUND(33.3266666666667*D3,2)

ROUND(33.3266666666667*1,2)

ROUND(33.3266666666667,2)

33.33

 The intermediate values are displayed

7 Control Excel

Keep control of your worksheets, audit the formulas, and check for errors. Make backup copies, and use the automatic save and recover capabilities. You can also control Excel through startup switches; shortcuts; KeyTips for the Ribbon commands; the Quick Access and Mini Toolbars.

106	**Audit Formulas**
108	**Protect Formulas**
109	**Check for Errors**
111	**Backup**
112	**AutoSave and AutoRecover**
113	**Startup Switches**
114	**Create a Shortcut**
115	**Ribbon Key Tips**
116	**Using Key Tips**
118	**Collapse the Ribbon**
119	**Quick Access Toolbar**
120	**Mini Toolbar**
121	**Print Worksheets**

Audit Formulas

When you are reviewing a worksheet and the formulas it contains, use the tools in the **Formula Auditing** group.

Don't forget

Precedents are those cells that are referred to by the formula in the selected cell.

Beware

The cell you select must contain a formula for the **Trace Precedents** button to operate.

 1 Click the **Formulas** tab, to see the **Formula Auditing** group

 2 If the commands are grayed, click the **File** tab, select **Excel Options**, then click **Advanced**

3 In the **Display options for this workbook** section, make sure that the **All** option is selected

 4 Select a cell, and click the **Trace Precedents** button in the **Formula Auditing** group

5 With a cell where there is no formula, such as B3, you receive a message

 6 With a cell that does contain a formula, such as E9, the arrow and box show the cells that are directly referred to by that formula

	A	B	C	D	E
1			Sales Invoice		
2	Item	Price	Discount	Quantity	Cost
3	DVD	49.99	1/3	1	33.33
4	CD	19.99	1/3	1	13.33
5	Book	16.99	1/3	1	11.33
6	Pad	1.39	1/3	10	9.27
7	Flash	13.99	1/3	7	65.29
8	Gizmo	11.19	1/3	1	7.46
9	TOTAL				140.01

E9 =SUM(E3:E8)

Click **Trace Precedents**, to see the next level of cells (if the first level of precedent cells refer to more cells)

8 Click the **Trace Dependents** button, to show the cells that rely on the value in the selected cell

9 Click the **Remove Arrows** button, in **Formula Auditing**

Dependents are those cells that contain formulas that refer to the selected cell.

You can analyze the role of cells that contain only literal values:

1 Click a cell – e.g. B2 – that contains no formula, and click **Trace Dependents**

2 If there are no cell references, you receive a warning message

3 Select B3, and click **Trace Dependents** three times to see the references to that cell

If you press **Trace Dependents** multiple times you can see the direct and the indirect references to the value in the selected cell.

107

Protect Formulas

Hot tip

This is the same action as performed by the keyboard shortcut **Ctrl** + ` (the grave accent key).

Don't forget

You can select ranges of cells, to protect multiple formulas at once.

Hot tip

When you print the worksheet with the formulas revealed, ensure you include the column and row headings. Select the **Page Layout** tab, and click **Print Headings** in the **Sheet Options** group.

---

1 Click **Show Formulas** on the **Formulas** tab, to display the formulas in the worksheet

2 To hide a formula, select the cell, then click the **Home** tab, **Format**, and **Format Cells...**

3 Click the **Protection** tab then click in the box labeled **Hidden**, and then click **OK**

4 Select the **Home** tab, **Format** and then **Protect Sheet...** to display the associated sheet panel then click **OK** to activate protection

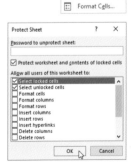

The cell's formula is no longer shown on the Formula Bar, and will be hidden when you choose the **Show Formulas** command.

Check for Errors

Excel applies rules to check for potential errors in formulas:

1 Click the **File** tab, select **Options**, then click **Formulas**

Hot tip

Some errors will just be warnings, and some may be due to information not yet recorded.

2 Select or clear the check boxes, to change the errors that Excel will detect

3 Select **Formulas**, and click the arrow on **Error Checking**, in the **Formula Auditing** group

4 Click **Error Checking...**, to review errors one by one, making corrections on the Formula Bar

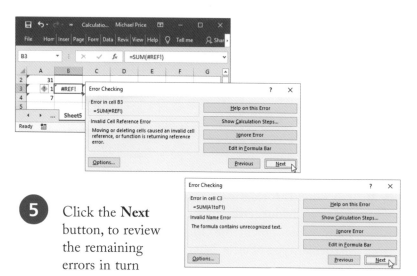

Beware

If the worksheet has previously been checked, any **Ignored** errors will not appear until you press the **Reset Ignored Errors** button, in **File**, **Excel Options**, **Formulas**.

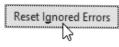

5 Click the **Next** button, to review the remaining errors in turn

...cont'd

You can also review individual errors on the worksheet:

1 Click an error, and then select **Trace Error**, from the **Error Checking** menu in **Formula Auditing**

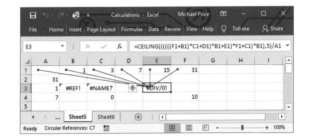

2 You can select **Circular References**, to see the cells that refer to their own contents, directly or indirectly

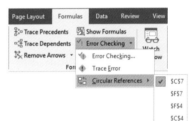

3 Click a cell from the list, to switch to that location

4 Press **F9** to recalculate the worksheet, and the cells involved in the circular references will be identified

5 Click the **Information** button on an individual error, to see more options, tailored to that particular type of error being reviewed

Backup

1 To make a copy of your workbook, click the **File** tab and select **Open** (or press the **Ctrl + O** shortcut key)

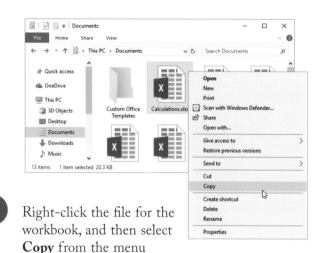

When you are working on a large worksheet it is often helpful to make a copy before you apply significant changes, so that you can undo them, if necessary.

2 Right-click the file for the workbook, and then select **Copy** from the menu

You can keep extra copies of your workbooks in your OneDrive (see pages 180-181).

3 Switch to the backup folder, right-click an empty area, and then select **Paste**

4 The file is copied to the folder, and you are warned if there's already a copy in the backup folder

If there's already a copy, Windows compares the two versions and lets you choose to replace the file, or skip copying the workbook.

5 Compare file info to confirm which version you want

AutoSave and AutoRecover

To review and adjust the **AutoRecover** and **AutoSave** settings:

 Click the **File** tab, then click **Options**, and select **Save**

Hot tip

Excel will automatically save your worksheet periodically, and can recover the file if your system shuts down in the middle of an update.

Hot tip

The **Document Recovery** task pane displays up to three versions of your file, with the most recent at the top.

Don't forget

Excel will keep the last **AutoSave** version, even when you deliberately close without saving, so you can still recover your latest changes.

 Check the **Save AutoRecover information** box, review the frequency, then click **OK** to save any changes

If your system shuts down without saving the current changes, the next time you start up Windows and Excel, you'll be given the opportunity to recover your changes, as recorded up to the last **AutoSave**.

Select a recovered entry, click the arrow and choose **Open, Save As...** or **Delete** as appropriate

Alternatively, select the original version to discard changes

Startup Switches

When you start Excel in the usual way, the Excel splash screen is displayed, and the Excel Start screen then opens where you can select a new blank workbook, a recent workbook or a template.

Hot tip

Excel 2019 normally opens at the Excel Start screen, but you can bypass this if you wish.

To start Excel without displaying the splash screen or the selection panel, use the **Run** command:

1 Press the **Windows key + R**, type **excel.exe /e**, and then press **Enter**

Hot tip

You can create a shortcut to Excel, with your required parameters, and place this on the Desktop or the Taskbar.

2 Select the **File** tab to create a new workbook or open an existing workbook

You can specify a workbook path and name and have Excel start with that workbook. For example, you might type a command such as **excel.exe /e "e:mydata\mybudget.xlsx"** into the **Run** box.

Don't forget

Use this method to start Excel in safe mode by typing **excel.exe /safe**. This can be useful if you are having problems opening a particular workbook.

Create a Shortcut

To create a shortcut to load Excel using the Startup switches discussed on page 113:

1 Locate the **Excel.exe** file on your hard drive, typically at **C:\Program Files (x86)\Microsoft Office\root\Office16\Excel.exe**

2 Right-click the Desktop, and then select **New, Shortcut**

3 Browse to the **Excel.exe** file location and select it, then add the required switch (e.g. **/e** or **/safe**) outside the quote marks

4 Name the new shortcut and click **Finish** to create a shortcut icon on the Desktop

5 Right-click the shortcut icon on the Desktop, and then select **Pin to taskbar** (or **Pin to Start**)

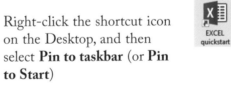

6 Select the entry to launch the program using the Startup switches

7 Right-click the entry to unpin

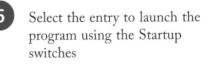

You can use the same process to create a shortcut that loads Excel with a specific workbook opened ready to use.

Hot tip

If necessary, use Windows Search to locate the **Excel.exe** program, and then note the location.

Beware

Make sure that you enter a space between the final quote mark and the command-line switch.

Ribbon Key Tips

Although the Ribbon is designed for mouse and touch selection, it is still possible to carry out any task available on the Ribbon without moving your hands from the keyboard.

If you hold down the **Alt** key for a couple of seconds, the Key Tips will display. Click **F10** to hide them, temporarily.

 Press and release the **Alt** key (or press the **F10** key) to show Key Tips (the keyboard shortcuts for the Ribbon)

The Key Tips change when you select a tab, and further Key Tips display when you select specific commands.

 Press the letter for the command tab that you want to display. For example, press **W** for **View**

It doesn't matter if **Alt** is pressed or not – the shortcut keys in the Key Tips will still operate. You can also use uppercase or lowercase.

 Press the letter(s) for the command or group that you want. For example, press **ZS** for **Show/Hide**

Using Key Tips

Hot tip

You can go to a cell, using keystrokes only.

Beware

The action associated with a particular letter may change, as you switch to another command tab or command group. For example, **N** can be the **Insert** tab, or **New window** in **View**.

 1 To go to a specific cell – **C7**, for example – press these keys:

Alt

H

FD

G

C7

Enter

2 The active cell changes to **C7**, the cell address that was required

...cont'd

3 With C7 selected, to insert **AutoSum**, press these keys:

Alt

H

Hot tip

You can insert the **AutoSum** function into the active cell using keystrokes only.

ZE

Hot tip

ZE expands the **Editing** group, but you can bypass this and go straight to **U** (**AutoSum**) if you don't need the visual prompt.

U

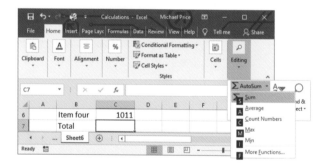

117

S

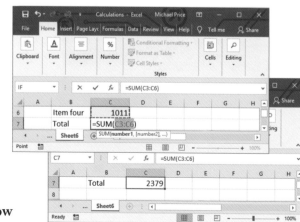

Don't forget

For tasks that you perform often, the Key Tips option can become the quickest way to operate, as you become familiar with the keystrokes needed.

Enter

Up arrow

Collapse the Ribbon

  Right-click the Ribbon, Tab Bar, or Quick Access Toolbar and select **Collapse the Ribbon**, or click **Ribbon Display Options** and select **Show Tabs**

Hot tip

You can also double-click the current tab, or press keys **Ctrl + F1**, or click the Collapse button on the corner, to collapse the Ribbon.

Don't forget

To redisplay the Ribbon, double-click the current tab, or press keys **Ctrl + F1**, or select **Show Tabs and Commands**, or simply click the Pin on the temporarily expanded Ribbon.

Hot tip

When you close down Excel with the Ribbon collapsed, it will still be collapsed when Excel restarts. When the Ribbon is fully displayed at closedown, it will be displayed on restart.

  2️⃣ With the Ribbon minimized, single-click a tab to display the Ribbon temporarily, to select commands from that tab

  3️⃣ The **Alt** key and the Key Tips still operate, even when you have the Ribbon minimized

Quick Access Toolbar

The Quick Access Toolbar contains a set of commands that are independent of the particular Command tab being displayed. Initially, there are three commands (**Save**, **Undo**, and **Redo**) plus a **Customize** button, but you can add other commands. By default, the Quick Access Toolbar is located above the **File** tab, but you can move it below the Ribbon.

 Right-click the Command tab bar, and select **Show Quick Access Toolbar Below the Ribbon**

Hot tip

When you select the entry, the instruction on the menu is modified to show the reverse process.

 To restore the default, right-click the Command tab bar, and select **Show Quick Access Toolbar Above the Ribbon**

3 To add a command, click **Customize Quick Access Toolbar**

4 Choose a command from the list, or select **More Commands...**

5 Choose a command category, select a command, click **Add** then click **OK** to place that command on the toolbar

Don't forget

You can also right-click any command on the Ribbon, then select **Add to Quick Access Toolbar** from the menu.

Mini Toolbar

The Mini Toolbar appears when you select text, or when editing the contents of a cell (and also when working with charts and text boxes). It offers quick access to the tools you need for text editing, such as font, size, style, alignment, color, and bullets. To see the Mini Toolbar:

1 Choose a cell with text content, enter Edit mode by pressing **F2**, and then select (highlight) part of the text

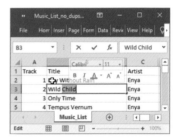

2 The Mini Toolbar appears above the cell, but may initially be very faint and quite transparent

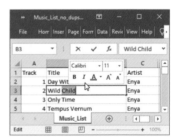

3 Move the mouse pointer towards the Mini Toolbar and the image strengthens

4 When the mouse pointer moves over the Mini Toolbar, the image solidifies and the toolbar is activated

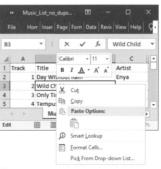

5 Move the mouse pointer away from the toolbar, and the image fades and may disappear

The Mini Toolbar feature was created as an extension of the context (right-click) menu, and it may appear whenever that menu appears.

6 Select a cell containing text, press **F2**, and right-click the cell to see the Mini Toolbar above the context menu

120

Print Worksheets

To preview printing for multiple worksheets:

 1   Open the workbook, and click the tab for the first sheet

2   To select adjacent sheets, hold down the **Shift** key, and click the tab for the last sheet in the group

3   To add other, non-adjacent sheets, hold down the **Ctrl** key and click the tabs for all of the other sheets required

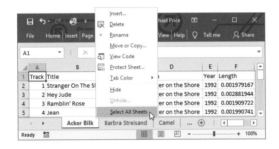

4   To select all the sheets, right-click any tab, then click **Select All Sheets**

5   Click the **File** tab, and select **Print**, to see the **Printer** details and the various settings

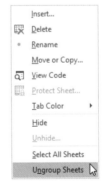

6   Alternatively, you can press the keyboard shortcut: **Ctrl + F2**

7   If you prefer to use Key Tips shortcuts, press **Alt F P V**

The **Preview** pane shows previews of the print pages for the sheets that you selected.

If you change any cell while multiple sheets are selected, the change is automatically applied to all selected sheets.

When multiple sheets are selected, the term **[Group]** appears on the Excel Title Bar.

To cancel the selection, click any unselected tab, or right-click any tab and click **Ungroup Sheets**.

...cont'd

Review the print preview pages before sending to the printer:

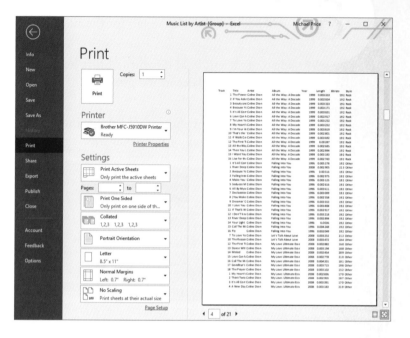

Click the **Page Setup** link to make detailed changes to the print settings. Click the **Printer Properties** link to control the printer.

If the settings are already as you want them, you can use the **Quick Print** button (see page 33) to start the **Print**, without previewing.

 Click the **Next Page** arrow to go forward, or the **Previous Page** arrow to go back

 Click the **Show Margins** button, to display margins. Click and drag the margins to adjust their positions

 Click the **Zoom to Page** button to switch the preview between close-up and full-page views

 Click the **Settings** options to adjust items such as paper size, orientation, scaling, and collation

 Click the **Printer** button to check the different printer options available

 Click the **Print** button to carry out the actual printing of the selected sheets

8 Charts

Excel makes it easy to turn your worksheet data into a chart. You can apply formatting, change the type, reselect the data, and add effects, such as 3-D display. Special chart types allow you to display data for stocks and shares. You can print the completed charts on their own, or as part of the worksheet.

124 Create a Chart

126 Recommended Chart Type

127 Change Chart Layout

128 Legend and Data Table

129 Change Chart Type

130 Pie Chart

132 3-D Pie Chart

133 3-D Column Chart

134 Share Price Data

135 Line Chart

136 Stock Chart

137 Mixed Types

138 Print Charts

Create a Chart

The following information about share purchases and prices will be used for the purpose of illustrating the Excel charting features:

- Total value of shares in portfolio at start of each year (to chart)
- The individual prices of the shares on those dates (to calculate)
- The total number of shares held (kept constant for simplicity)

Hot tip

To create a chart you can modify and format later, start by entering the data on a worksheet. Then, select the data and choose the chart type.

Don't forget

If the cells you want are not in a continuous range, you can select non-adjacent cells, or ranges, as long as the final selection forms a rectangle. You can also hide rows or columns that you don't need.

	A	B	C	D	E	F	G	H	I	J	K	L	M	N	O	P
1	Portfolio Valuation										Share Prices					
2	Date	AAPL	BT	IBM	MSFT	RYCEY	WMT		Total		AAPL	BT	IBM	MSFT	RYCEY	WMT
3	1/1/2005	98.87	99.03	93.42	78.84	99.80	52.40		522.36		5.49	19.81	93.42	26.28	4.99	52.40
4	1/1/2006	194.17	91.88	81.30	84.45	157.60	46.11		655.50		10.79	18.38	81.30	28.15	7.88	46.11
5	1/1/2007	220.45	152.60	99.15	92.58	187.00	47.69		799.47		12.25	30.52	99.15	30.86	9.35	47.69
6	1/1/2008	348.07	129.62	107.11	97.80	191.60	50.74		924.94		19.34	25.92	107.11	32.60	9.58	50.74
7	1/1/2009	231.76	38.10	91.65	51.30	94.64	47.12		554.57		12.88	7.62	91.65	17.10	4.73	47.12
8	1/1/2010	493.87	54.43	122.39	84.54	152.60	53.43		961.25		27.44	10.89	122.39	28.18	7.63	53.43
9	1/1/2011	872.54	70.75	162.00	83.19	204.84	56.07		1449.39		48.47	14.15	162.00	27.73	10.24	56.07
10	1/1/2012	1173.81	80.80	192.60	88.59	231.40	61.36		1828.56		65.21	16.16	192.60	29.53	11.57	61.36
11	1/1/2013	1171.26	98.65	203.07	82.35	299.84	69.95		1925.12		65.07	19.73	203.07	27.45	14.99	69.95
12	1/1/2014	1287.26	157.63	176.68	113.52	390.52	74.68		2200.28		71.51	31.53	176.68	37.84	19.53	74.68
13	1/1/2015	2108.88	156.95	153.31	121.20	270.44	84.98		2895.76		117.16	31.39	153.31	40.40	13.52	84.98
14	1/1/2016	1752.12	174.30	124.79	165.27	160.60	66.36		2443.44		97.34	34.86	124.79	55.09	8.03	66.36
15	1/1/2017	2184.30	96.80	174.52	193.95	169.80	66.74		2886.11		121.35	19.36	174.52	64.65	8.49	66.74
16	1/1/2018	3013.74	93.80	163.70	285.03	250.80	106.60		3913.67		167.43	18.76	163.70	95.01	12.54	106.60
17											Share Quantities					
18											18	5	1	3	20	1

Select the Data

Some chart types, such as pie and bubble charts, require a specific data arrangement. For most chart types, however, including line, column, and bar charts, you can use the data as arranged in the rows and columns of the worksheet.

Hot tip

If you let Excel choose the data, ensure there is a blank row and column between the data you want to plot, and other data on the worksheet.

1 Select the cells that contain the data that you want to use for the chart

2 Alternatively, click any cell in a block of data and let Excel select the whole block

	A	B	C	D	E	F	G
2	Date	AAPL	BT	IBM	MSFT	RYCEY	WMT
3	1/1/2005	98.87	99.03	93.42	78.84	99.80	52.40
4	1/1/2006	194.17	91.88	81.30	84.45	157.60	46.11
5	1/1/2007	220.45	152.60	99.15	92.58	187.00	47.69
6	1/1/2008	348.07	129.62	107.11	97.80	191.60	50.74
7	1/1/2009	231.76	38.10	91.65	51.30	94.64	47.12
8	1/1/2010	493.87	54.43	122.39	84.54	152.60	53.43
9	1/1/2011	872.54	70.75	162.00	83.19	204.84	56.07
10	1/1/2012	1173.81	80.80	192.60	88.59	231.40	61.36
11	1/1/2013	1171.26	98.65	203.07	82.35	299.84	69.95
12	1/1/2014	1287.26	157.63	176.68	113.52	390.52	74.68
13	1/1/2015	2108.88	156.95	153.31	121.20	270.44	84.98
14	1/1/2016	1752.12	174.30	124.79	165.27	160.60	66.36
15	1/1/2017	2184.30	96.80	174.52	193.95	169.80	66.74
16	1/1/2018	3013.74	93.80	163.70	285.03	250.80	106.60

3 Click the **Insert** tab, and then select a chart type (**Column**, for example) from the **Charts** group

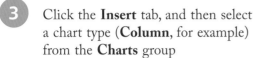

4 Choose the chart subtype – e.g. **2-D Stacked Column** (to show how each share contributes to the total value)

5 The chart is superimposed over the data on the worksheet, and **Chart Tools** (**Design**, **Layout**, and **Format** tabs) are added to the Ribbon

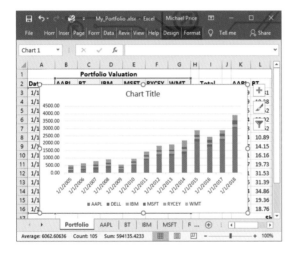

6 Click **Move Chart**, in the **Location** group on the **Design** tab, to choose where you want the chart to be placed. For example, choose **New sheet** to create a separate chart sheet, and accept the default name of "Chart1" (or provide your preferred name)

Hot tip

When you move the mouse pointer over any of the chart subtypes, you get a description and an indication of when that chart subtype might prove useful.

Stacked Column

Use this chart type to:
• Compare parts of a whole.
• Show how parts of a whole change over time.

Don't forget

You can also move the chart on the worksheet, by clicking on the border and dragging it to another part of the worksheet.

125

Recommended Chart Type

Excel will recommend chart types for your selected data:

 Click the **Recommended Charts** button (or click the arrow on the corner of the **Charts** group)

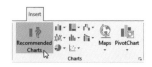

The **Recommended Charts** button lets you pick from a variety of charts that are right for your data.

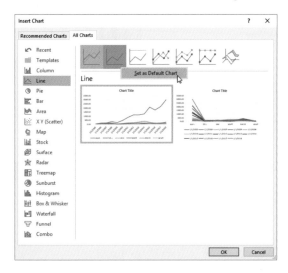

 Click the **All Charts** tab to see the range of charts

The usual default chart type is a **2-D Clustered Column**, which uses vertical rectangles to compare values across categories.

The **2-D Stacked Line** chart selected as the new default shows the trend in the contribution, from each of the categories.

Right-click any chart type and select **Set as Default Chart** from the context menu

With a data range selected, press **F11** and the default chart type is displayed on a chart sheet, using the next free name ("Chart1" in this case)

Change Chart Layout

Hot tip

Select **Quick Layout** from **Chart Layouts** to quickly try out some predefined chart layouts.

1 Select the **Design** tab **Chart Layouts** group and click **Add Chart Element**

2 Select **Chart Title** and choose the position; e.g. **Above Chart**

3 Right-click the sample words "Chart Title", then select **Edit Text**, to amend the wording, and **Font** to amend its style

Don't forget

In the same way, you can add **Axis Titles** and adjust the **Gridlines**.

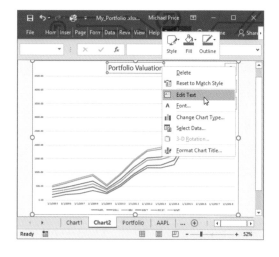

Hot tip

Instead of typing the titles directly, link to a cell on the worksheet. Click in the title, type = on the Formula Bar, select the cell with the text, then press **Enter**.

127

Legend and Data Table

 Select **Design**, **Add Chart Element**, **Legend** and choose its position (and alignment) on the chart; e.g. **Right**

The **Legend** provides the key to the entries on the chart; in this case, the stock symbols for all of the shares.

You can also display data labels, to show the data values at each point on the lines.

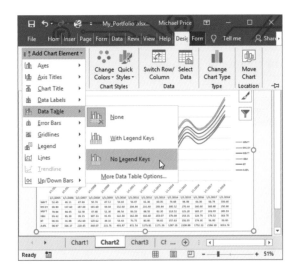

 To show the full details, click **Data Table**, and choose the options, such as where to position the table, and whether to display legend keys

If you show the data for the chart in a table and include **Legend** keys, you can then select **None** to turn off the display of the **Legend** itself.

Again, you can adjust the text size and style for the entries in the **Legend** and the **Data Table**

Change Chart Type

1 Select the **Design** tab, and click **Change Chart Type** from the **Type** group

2 In the **Change Chart Type** dialog, select the chart type and subtype (for example, chart type **Area** and subtype **Stacked Area**), then click **OK**

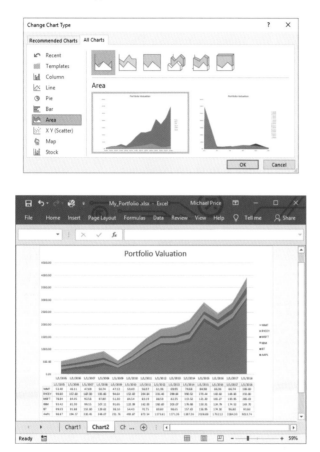

Excel 2019 adds two new chart types. **Filled Map** charts recognize data such as countries or states, and display data on an appropriate map.

State	Population
CA	39536653
TX	28304596
FL	20984400
NY	19849399
PA	12805537
IL	12802023
OH	11658609
GA	10429379
NC	10273419

Funnel charts are meant to display progressively decreasing values.

3 The **Design**, **Chart Styles** group allows you to change the colors and the overall visual style for your chart

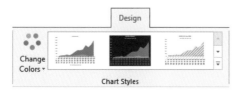

When you change the chart style, you may need to apply other changes such as text font sizes.

Pie Chart

Hot tip

A **Pie Chart** compares the contributions of individual items to the total. This is intended for a single set of data, such as a year's share values.

NEW

Excel 2019 will first load a placeholder for large charts and then load text right away – so you can start editing without delay.

Don't forget

This layout shows the data labels and the relative percentage contributions to the total value, shown on the pie chart segments, rather than using a separate legend box.

1 Select the data labels and one set of data in an adjacent row (or hold down **Ctrl** to select non-adjacent cells)

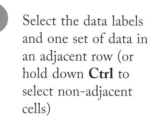

2 Click the **Insert** tab, select **Pie** from the **Charts** group, and choose the chart type – the standard **2-D Pie Chart**, for example

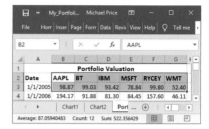

3 Click the **Design** tab, and select **Move Chart**, to create a chart sheet – named "Chart3", for example

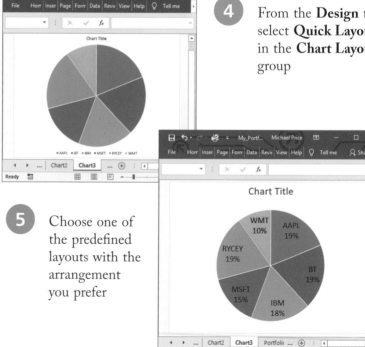

4 From the **Design** tab select **Quick Layout**, in the **Chart Layouts** group

5 Choose one of the predefined layouts with the arrangement you prefer

...cont'd

You can also change the data series selected for the chart:

1 Select the **Chart Tools Design** tab, and then click **Select Data**, in the **Data** group

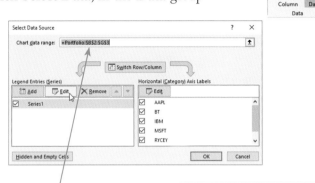

2 Here, the data range is for 2005. Click the data selection (usually "Series1"), and then click the **Edit** button

3 Click the **Collapse** button and select a new data range, such as the 2012 values, then click the **Expand** button

4 Click OK to update the pie chart for the new period

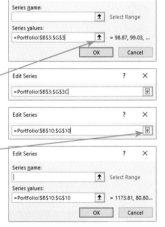

You can also right-click the chart and choose **Select Data...**, to modify the data source settings.

131

Note how Excel decides where to put the data label, moving it outside the segment if the text won't fit into the space available.

3-D Pie Chart

One of the subtypes for the pie chart offers a 3-D view.

 Select the **Chart Tools Design** tab, click **Change Chart Type**, select **Pie**, **3-D Pie**, and then click **OK**

In a 3-D pie chart, it is the chart segments that are displayed in 3-D format, rather than the data itself (hence the grayed Z component).

② Right-click the chart, select **3-D Rotation**, then set rotation values (e.g. X: 270°, Y: 30°, Perspective: 15°), then click **Close**

③ The information is presented in 3-D display form. You can select **Chart Tools, Format** to adjust the appearance; e.g. to add a background color

Experiment with the rotation and format options, to find the most effective presentation form for your data.

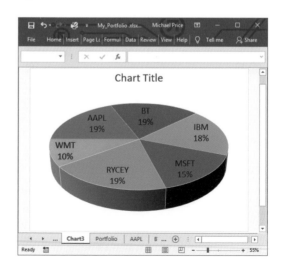

3-D Column Chart

A true 3-D chart has three sets of values to plot, giving three axes. In the example data, these are "Shares", "Values", and "Dates".

1 Select the data, click **Insert**, **Charts**, **Column**, and select the **3-D Column** chart type

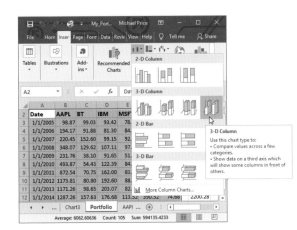

The **3-D Area** chart also presents data using three axes, to give a true 3-D representation.

2 Select **Chart Tools**, **Design**, and **Format**, to make the desired adjustments to the appearance. Right-click and select **3-D Rotation** to change orientation and perspective

3 Right-click the chart and choose **Move Chart**, then select **New sheet** named as, say, "Chart4"

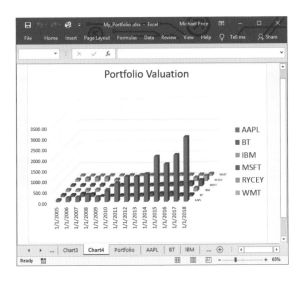

Click **Chart Tools**, **Design**, **Select Data**, and click the **Switch Row/Column** button to exchange the horizontal and depth axes, to give a different view of the data.

Share Price Data

Don't forget

The share prices in a portfolio worksheet could be taken from price history tables downloaded from the Yahoo! Finance website.

 1 Go to **finance.yahoo.com**, search for the stock symbol (**MSFT**, for example), then click the **Historical Data** link

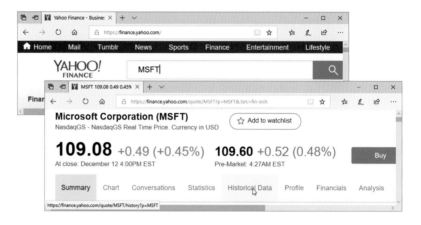

Don't forget

The price history table from **Yahoo! Finance** provides information in reverse date sequence, on a daily, weekly, or monthly basis. Use the **Adjusted Close** values to ensure that the prices are comparable over time.

2 Specify the **Time Period** and the **Frequency** and click **Apply**, then click **Download Data** and save the CSV file

Import the data into a spreadsheet (see pages 42-43) to use in a lookup table, as shown below.

Hot tip

See pages 72-73 for details on converting a range into an Excel table. See page 90 for an example of using the **HLOOKUP** function.

The data for other stock symbols is downloaded and imported in a similar manner.

Line Chart

The charts, so far, have used just a few dates from the tables. The complete tables, however, provide a continuous view of the data.

 1 The **Historical** worksheet contains the date column and adjusted closing price column for each of the shares

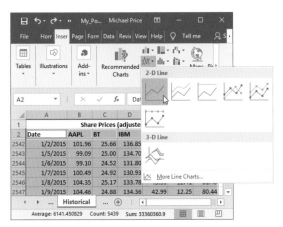

Note that for ease-of-display purposes, the rows for years 2004-2014 have been hidden, so the chart will be for 2015-2018 only.

2 Select the data, click **Insert, Chart and Line**, then choose the **2-D Line** chart subtype, to get a plot for each share

3 Right-click the chart and choose **Move Chart**, then select **New sheet** as, say, "Chart5"

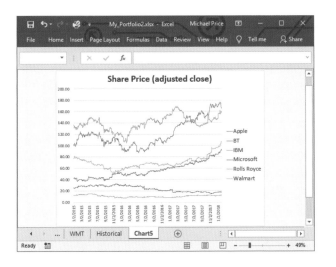

Hot tip

You can choose line, stacked line, or 100% stacked line (with or without markers). There's also a **3-D Line**, but this is just a perspective view, not three axes of data.

Don't forget

As with all the charts, you can move this chart to a separate chart sheet and adjust position and styles for the titles and the legend.

Stock Chart

The downloaded share data can also be used for a special type of chart, known as the **Stock** chart.

 From the shares table, filter the data (e.g. for 2017), and then select the columns for **Date**, **Open**, **High**, **Low**, and **Close**

Beware

This chart type requires data in a specific layout for the chart subtype; e.g. **High-Low-Close** or **Open-High-Low-Close** (and the date values can be used as data labels).

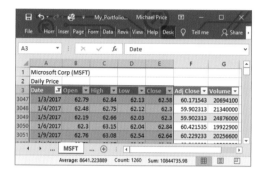

Open **Insert Chart** (see page 126), select **Stock** charts, select type **Open-High-Low-Close**, then click **OK**

The prices are plotted, with lines for high/low, hollow boxes for increases, and solid boxes for decreases

Hot tip

Move the chart to a separate chart sheet, add titles, and format the titles and the legend. Right-click the axis, and select **Format Axis** to change the minimum and maximum, to emphasize the price spreads.

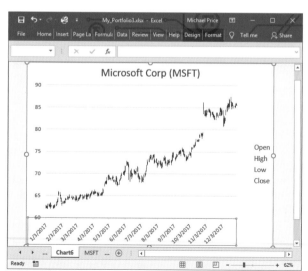

Mixed Types

You can have more than one type of chart displayed at the same time, as in the **Volume** subtypes of the **Stock** chart.

1 Move **Volume** to the location between **Date** and **Open**

2 Select the headings and the data (for year 2017)

3 **Insert** the **Stock** chart, choosing type **Volume-Open-High-Low-Close**

4 The chart uses two vertical axes, to show the volumes and the various price values

Hot tip

You need to rearrange the data downloaded from Yahoo! Finance to create the volume Stock charts, since volumes must be listed before the various share prices.

Don't forget

In this example, the two types of chart use the same horizontal values (dates). When necessary, however, Excel will specify a secondary horizontal axis.

Print Charts

When you have an embedded chart in your worksheet, it prints as positioned, along with the data, when you select **Print** from the **File** tab and click the **Print** button. To print the chart on its own:

 Select the chart, then select the **File** tab and click **Print**

The chart may obscure part of the data. Switch to **Page Break Preview**, and drag the chart, to reposition it before printing the worksheet.

 An extra "Print what" option (**Selected Chart**) appears, and the other options are grayed, so only the chart will print

When the chart is in a separate chart sheet, you can print it on its own, or as part of the workbook, just as you print a worksheet.

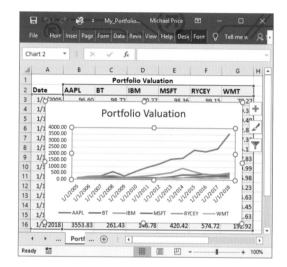

9 Macros in Excel

If there are tasks that you carry out frequently, you can define the actions required, as a macro. You can assign the macro to a key combination, or to an icon on the toolbar, to make it easy to reuse. However, you must make sure that security is in place to prevent abuse.

140 Macros

141 Create Macros

142 Record a Macro

144 Apply the Macro

145 View the Macro

146 Macro to Make a Table

148 Edit the Macro

149 Use the Macro

150 Create Macros with VBA

152 Add Macros to the Toolbar

154 Debug Macros

Beware

Macros are powerful, but they can be subject to misuse. Microsoft has included security checks and limitations in Excel to authenticate macros, and to help prevent them being introduced into your system and run without your knowledge.

Don't forget

To check which type of workbook you have open, tell Windows to reveal the file type (see pages 37-38).

Beware

Enable all macros is not recommended as a permanent setting. Select a more restricted level as soon as you have finished creating or changing the macros stored in your active workbook.

Macros

Any task in Excel may be performed by a "macro". Macros are often used to carry out simple but repetitive tasks, such as entering your name and address, or inserting a standard piece of text. In other cases, macros may be used for complex and involved tasks, difficult to reproduce accurately without some kind of help.

To create a macro, carry out an example of the actions, with Excel recording the keystrokes involved as you complete the task. The sequence is stored as a macro in the **Visual Basic for Applications** (VBA) programming language. You can edit your recorded macro, or create new macros, using the Visual Basic Editor.

Macros can be very powerful, because they are able to run commands on your computer. For this reason, Microsoft Excel prevents the default Excel 2019 file format (file type **.xlsx**) from storing VBA macro code. Therefore, the recommended place for storing the macros you create is in your hidden **Personal Macro Workbook**, and this is the method used for the examples in the following pages. If you share macros, they need to be stored in the workbooks that use them. These workbooks must then be saved in the Excel 2019 macro-enabled file format (file type **.xlsm**). You may need to reset the security level, temporarily, to enable all macros, so that you can work on macros in the active workbook:

1 Select the **File** tab, **Options**, **Trust Center**, then click the **Trust Center Settings...** and select **Macro Settings**

2 Check the setting to enable all macros, then click **OK**

Create Macros

To display the commands for recording and viewing macros:

 Select the **View** tab, and click the arrow below the **Macros** button, in the **Macros** group

 You can choose to view or record macros, and choose between relative or absolute cell references (a toggle setting)

These options are also available from the **Developer** tab, along with the **Macro Security** and **Visual Basic** commands. By default, this tab is not displayed. To add the **Developer** tab to the Ribbon:

 Click the **File** tab, and then select **Options** (or press the keys **Alt F T**) and choose **Customize Ribbon**

 Click the **Developer** box in the **Main Tabs** section, and the **Developer** tab will be added to the Tab Bar

Don't forget

Selecting the **Macros** button, rather than the arrow, has the same effect as selecting the **View Macros** entry.

141

Hot tip

You can record, view, and edit macros, using commands from either the **View** tab or the **Developer** tab, but to create macros from scratch, or to change security settings, you will need to use the **Developer** tab.

Record a Macro

Assume that you need to add some standard disclaimer text to a number of workbooks. To create a macro for this:

1 Open a blank workbook, and click in cell A1

2 Select the **Developer** tab, then from the **Code** group click the **Use Relative References** button and the **Record Macro** button – to open the **Record Macro** dialog box

3 Enter a name for the Macro name, and specify a shortcut key; e.g. **Shift + D** (the **Ctrl** key will be added automatically)

4 Select **Personal Macro Workbook** (the preferred location to store macros), add a description, then click **OK** to start the recording

5 Carry out the required actions, then select the **Developer** tab and from the **Code** group, click **Stop Recording**

To check out the macro:

 Click in a different cell (C4, for example) then press the **Shift** + **Ctrl** + **D** shortcut to try out the macro

If there are problems with the macro, you may be able to use the **Visual Basic Editor** to make the changes that are needed (see page 148).

 The text is entered into the worksheet, at the active cell

The start location changes, because the macro was created with relative references. However, if you click in any specific cells while the macro is being recorded, those references will be honored.

When you have finished checking the macro, close the workbook:

 Click the **File** tab, and select **Close**

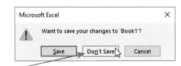

Select **Don't Save** when asked if you want to save your changes

The relative reference applies to the macro, as the initial cell was selected before macro recording was started.

The macro itself will be retained in the **Personal Macro Workbook**. This will be saved at the end of the Excel session (see page 144).

Active Workbook Macros

If you selected to store the recorded macro in the active workbook, you must save that workbook as file type **.xlsm**. You will also need to reset the level of macro security (see page 140).

When you close the active workbook, the macros it contains will no longer be available in that Excel session, unless you save it – as described on page 144.

Apply the Macro

The macro remains available throughout the Excel session, if you stored it in the Personal Macro Workbook, and you can apply it to any Excel workbook (.xlsm, .xlsx, or .xls). Once saved, it will be available to use in future sessions.

The workbook type does not need to be changed to .xlsm, since you are adding text to it, not the actual macro code.

If you choose not to save in the Personal Macro Workbook, any macros created during this Excel session will be lost. This can be a useful way of trying out new ideas, without commitment.

 1 Open a workbook that requires the disclaimer text, and select the location (e.g. My Personal Budget, cell A16)

2 Press the shortcut **Shift + Ctrl + D** to run the macro

3 Save the worksheet (no need to change the file type)

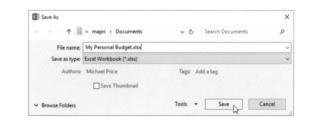

4 When you end the Excel session, you can save your **Personal Macro Workbook** and, with it, any macros that you have created during the session

View the Macro

1 Select the **View** tab; then, from the **Window** group, click the **Unhide** button

Don't forget

2 Select the workbook "PERSONAL.XLSB", which is your **Personal Macro Workbook**, then click **OK**

You can view and edit the macro. However, since it is stored in a hidden workbook, you must start by making the workbook visible.

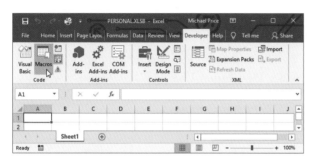

3 Click the **Developer** tab and from the **Code** group, select **Macros**

Hot tip

4 Select the macro you want to review and click **Edit**, to display the code in the **Visual Basic Editor**

You can make changes to the macro – e.g. revise the text that is entered into the cells – even if you don't know the VBA language.

145

```
Sub Disclaimer()
'
' Disclaimer Macro
' Disclaimer text
'
' Keyboard Shortcut: Ctrl+Shift+D
'
    ActiveCell.FormulaR1C1 = "This workbook is for training purposes only"
    ActiveCell.Offset(1, 0).Range("A1").Select
    ActiveCell.FormulaR1C1 = "The figures included are fictitious"
    ActiveCell.Offset(1, 0).Range("A1").Select
End Sub
```

Beware

When you've finished viewing or changing your macros, you should select **View**, **Hide**, to hide the **Personal Macro Workbook**.

5 Select **File, Save PERSONAL.XLSB** to save any changes, then **Close and Return to Microsoft Excel**

Macro to Make a Table

 Open a Share history file – "WMT.csv", for example

 Select **Developer**, **Use Relative References**, and then click **Record Macro**

Specify the macro name, shortcut key and description, then click **OK** to start the recording

The keystroke steps in the process are as follows:

1 Go to cell A3 (the start of the data range):
Alt H FD G A3 Enter

 Select the whole data range (A3:G255 in this example) using the end and arrows keys:
ShiftDown (press and hold down Shift key)
End RightArrow
End DownArrow
ShiftUp (release Shift key)

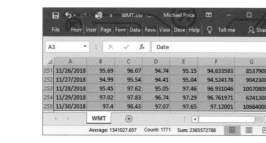

This shows the data range selected, ready for creating the Excel table.

3 Create an Excel Table from the selected set of data:
   Alt N T Enter

If the data column is in descending order it may be unsuitable for a lookup table.

In some cases, share history files are in descending sequence. To ensure ascending sequence, add these keystrokes:

4 Go to cell A4 (the date field in first row of actual data):
   Alt H FD G A4 Enter

5 Sort the column in ascending date sequence:
   Alt A SA

If you create an Excel table in a **.csv** file, you must save as Excel Workbook (**.xlsx** format), to retain the table (see page 149).

6 Click **Developer**, **Stop Recording** to finish the macro, then save the table as an Excel Workbook

Edit the Macro

 1 Unhide the **Personal Macro Workbook** (see page 145)

 2 Select **Developer**, then **Macros**, from the **Code** group

Hot tip

Check the recorded macro, to see if any changes are needed.

 3 Select the "Make_Share_Table" macro, and click **Edit**, to display the code in the **Visual Basic Editor**

Beware

148

You should hide the **Personal Macro Workbook** when you have finished making changes to the macro.

Don't forget

Sections of the macro may be specific to the original workbook. In this case, there are references to the worksheet name. These can be replaced with the generic reference to **ActiveSheet**.

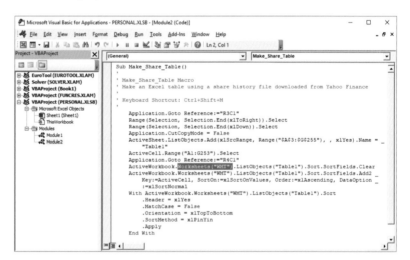

 4 Select **Edit**, **Replace**, to replace the text "Worksheets("WMT")" with "ActiveSheet", and click **Replace All**

5 To save the changes, select **File**, **Save PERSONAL.XLSB**, then select **File**, **Close and Return to Microsoft Excel**

Use the Macro

1 Open another Share history file; e.g. "RYCEY.csv"

This example has the data in descending sequence.

2 Press the macro shortcut key **Shift** + **Ctrl** + **M** to create an Excel table (with the data in ascending sequence)

3 Save the worksheet as file type **Excel Workbook (.xlsx)**

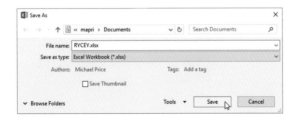

Repeat this for any other Share history files, which can each be converted to Excel table format with a single click of the **Make_Share_Table** macro shortcut key.

Follow a similar procedure to create and test macros for any other tasks that you need to complete on a regular basis.

Beware

As written, the macro assumes that the worksheet will have data in rows 4 to 255 (12/2017-12/2015). If there are fewer actual rows, the remainder will appear as empty table rows. Extra rows will be stored after the table.

Hot tip

The macro now refers to the **ActiveSheet**, so it converts the data range in the current worksheet, without regard to its name.

Don't forget

The macro remains in the **Personal Macro Workbook**, so the shared workbooks do not need to be macro-enabled.

Create Macros with VBA

 Display the **Developer** tab on the Ribbon (see page 141)

 Select the **Developer** tab, and then select **Visual Basic**

A list of album tracks is used here, to illustrate the use of Visual Basic to create a macro; in this case, to insert page breaks after each album.

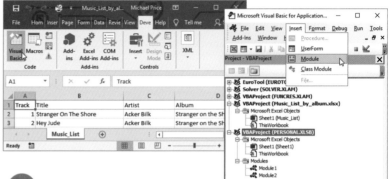

This macro identifies the last non-blank row in the worksheet. It checks the values in column 4 (Album name), and inserts a page break whenever the name changes.

 Click **VBAProject** for **PERSONAL.XLSB**, and then select **Insert, Module**

 In the code window for the module, type (or paste) the code for your macro

You can discover more about Visual Basic programming in our companion books, **Excel VBA in easy steps** and **Visual Basic in easy steps**.

When you have entered and checked the macro code, select **File, Close and Return to Microsoft Excel**

You can search on the internet for sample Visual Basic macros; e.g. at **code.msdn.microsoft.com**

6 In the "Music_List" worksheet, click the **Page Break Preview** button on the status bar, to see the page setup

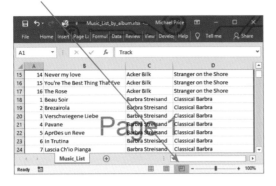

Here, the second album continues on the same page as the first. To apply page breaks based on albums:

1 Click the **Developer** tab **Macros** button

2 Select the **Page_Breaks** macro, and click **Run**

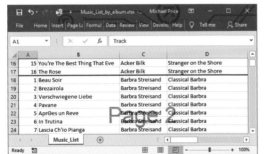

3 Manual page breaks are inserted at every change of album in the worksheet

151

4 Select **Page Layout**, **Print Titles**, and set **Rows to repeat at top** to the first row, so you get the headings on every print page

Add Macros to the Toolbar

If you specified a **Ctrl** or **Shift** + **Ctrl** shortcut when you created your macro, you can run the macro by pressing the appropriate key combination. You can also run the macro by clicking the **Macros** button, from the **View** tab or the **Developer** tab. To make macros more accessible, you can add the **View Macros** option to the Quick Access Toolbar:

You could also right-click the **Macros** button, and select **Add to Quick Access Toolbar**.

 Select **File**, **Options** and select **Quick Access Toolbar**, then **Popular Commands** in **Choose commands from**

2 Click **View Macros**, click **Add**, and click **OK**. **View Macros** now appears on the Quick Access Toolbar

If you want to add or change the shortcut key for a macro, select it by using the Macros button, and then click the Options button.

3 To run a macro, click the **View Macros** button on the toolbar, select the macro that you want, and click **Run**

Alternatively, you can add macros as individual icons on the Quick Access Toolbar. To do this:

 1 Open **Excel Options**, select **Quick Access Toolbar**, then **Macros** in **Choose commands from**

2 Scroll down to the particular macros, select each one in turn, and click **Add**

3 Each macro will have the same icon. You can click **Modify**, and select a different icon

4 The icons for each of the macros will be added to the Quick Access Toolbar

Hot tip

Macros can also be associated with graphics, or hot spots on the worksheet.

153

5 Hover the mouse pointer over an icon and the ScreenTip shows the name of the macro, which runs immediately when you click the icon

Debug Macros

If you are having a problem with a macro, or if you are just curious to see how it works, you can run it one step at a time:

 Select **Macros** from **Developer** (or from **View**), choose the macro you want to run, and click **Step Into**

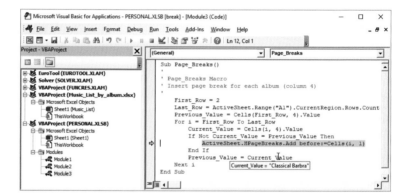

Open a worksheet for which the macro was written, before selecting the **Step Into** option.

 Press **F8** repeatedly to run through the code, one step at a time

154

 At any stage, hold the mouse over any variable, to see its current value

The breakpoint is the macro statement at which execution will automatically stop. The breakpoints you set will not be saved with the code when you exit.

Select **Debug**, to see the other testing options available, such as setting breakpoints

Press **F5** to continue to the next breakpoint (or to complete the macro, if no breakpoints are set)

To finish and leave Debug, select **File, Close and Return to Microsoft Excel**

10 Templates and Scenarios

For the most frequent uses of Excel, you'll find ready-made templates to give you a head start. There are more Excel resources at Microsoft Office Support and other websites. Excel also has special problem-solving tools.

156 Templates

158 Online Templates

160 More Excel Resources

162 What-If Analysis

164 Summary Reports

166 Goal Seek

167 Optimization

168 Project Worksheet

169 Solver

Templates

You can save effort, and you may discover new aspects of Excel, if you base your new workbooks on available templates.

1 Click the **File** tab, and then click **New** to be offered the blank workbook and suggestions for templates

Hot tip

You can also search for and select templates from the Start screen that normally displays when you start Excel.

2 Review the example templates, or select a category such as "Financial Management" to see more templates

3 Select the template you want to use – "Loan amortization schedule", for example; review the details, then click **Create**

Don't forget

The template will be downloaded and a workbook will be opened ready for use, though you can make any changes you wish, if it doesn't exactly meet your requirements.

4 The input boxes are predefined with data, so that you can check out the way the workbook operates

Hot tip

Review the data, and then make changes to the values, to see the effect. For example, change the payments per annum from 12 to 6.

5 Adjust the values, and the worksheet is extended by the number of payments, and displays the calculated amounts

6 To view the formulas behind the calculations, press **Ctrl** + ` (or select **Show Formulas** on the **Formulas** tab)

Don't forget

To keep the results, you need to save the workbook – the default name is the template name, with a number appended.

7 Select the **Formulas** tab and click the **Name Manager** button (or press **Ctrl + F3**), to see the names defined in the workbook, with their values and their cell references

Online Templates

To help in creating a workbook for a particular purpose, you can amend an existing template and save the revised copy in your **Custom Office Templates** library for later use:

1 Select **File**, **New** and click **Search for online templates**; enter a search term – e.g. "exercise" – and click the magnifier

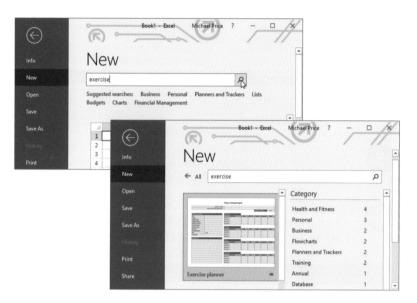

2 Matching templates will be listed, and a series of related subcategories offered, to help you focus on the topic

3 Scroll down and you will see that related templates from your other Office applications may also be detected

Choose a template, and create a new workbook (see page 156).

...cont'd

You can amend the selected template and save the revised copy in your Documents library for later use.

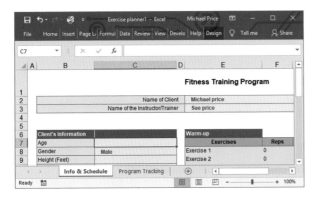

Hot tip

If the template contains macros or VB code, you will need to save it as an **Excel Macro-Enabled Template (*.xltm)**.

1 Select **File**, **Save As**, select your **Documents** folder and choose the type of **Excel Template (*.xltx)**

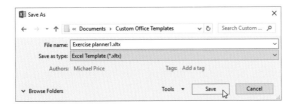

2 It will be saved in **Documents/Custom Office Templates**

3 Select **File**, **New**, **Personal** to view your templates

Don't forget

You can also save an Excel Workbook as a template to use as the basis for other workbooks. Such templates are also saved in the **Personal** area.

More Excel Resources

The internet is a prolific source of advice and guidance for Excel users at all levels. Here are some websites that may prove useful:

 1 Go to **support.office.com** and select the Excel icon

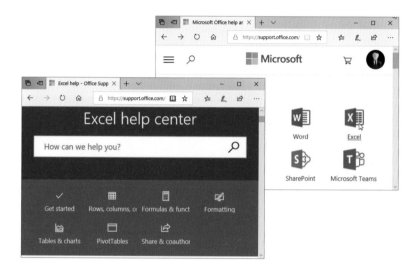

Don't forget

A search on **google.com** with Excel-related search terms will result in millions of matches, so it will be easier to start from a more focused website such as Microsoft Office Support.

 2 Review advice for getting started and using Excel

 3 Scroll on for links to Excel training, templates and tips

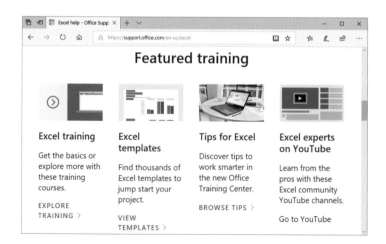

Beware

The actual links and content for the Office web pages change over time, but you should expect to find links similar to those shown.

4 Connect to the community of Excel experts on YouTube

...cont'd

5 Microsoft MVPs (most valued professionals) can also provide useful information. Go to **mvp.microsoft.com**

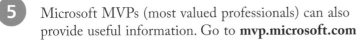
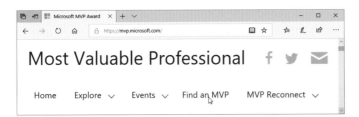

There is every possibility that your Excel question may have been answered previously on the community forum – use the Search box before repeating the question.

6 Select **Find an MVP**, then enter the **Keyword** "Excel" and pick an **Award Category** – e.g. "Office Apps & Services"

7 Enter your **Country or region**, and click **Search**, to see the list of your local specialists

If you are interested in creating Excel functions and macros, you should visit the Office and Excel developers' centers:

8 Go to **developer.microsoft.com/office** and select **Excel**

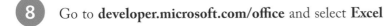
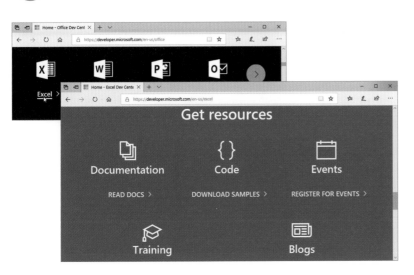

161

You'll find that many forum references relate to Excel 2016, 2013 or previous versions. These will often be just as applicable when you are running Excel 2019.

What-If Analysis

A **What-If Analysis** involves the process of changing values in cells, to see how those changes affect the outcome on the worksheet. A set of values that represent a particular outcome is known as a scenario. To create a scenario:

Sometimes you can set up your worksheet so that several outcomes are visible at once (as in the PMT example on page 93). You can get a similar effect by using a **What-If Analysis**, and defining scenarios.

In Excel 2019 you can easily create a new worksheet to forecast data trends using the **Forecast Sheet** option on the **Data** tab.

In this case, the scenarios explore the effects of making extra payments, with the first scenario having an extra payment of zero.

 Open the worksheet, and enter details for a loan; a 25-year mortgage, for example

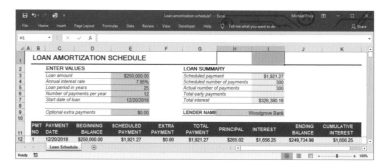

 Select the **Data** tab and, from the **Forecast** group, click **What-If Analysis**, then choose **Scenario Manager...**

 Click **Add**, type a scenario name (e.g. "X000"), enter the address references for the cells that you may want to change, and then click **OK**

 Change the scenario values; in this case, a gradually increasing value for **Scheduled_Extra_Payments**

...cont'd

5 Repeat steps 3 and 4 for each scenario, clicking **Add** then **OK**, incrementing each by 50 (i.e. names "X050"... "X350" and values 50.00...350.00)

6 When you've specified the last scenario, click **OK** to complete the process

Hot tip

Additional input cells (**LoanAmount** and **LoanPeriod**) have been selected. They have been left unchanged for these scenarios, but give the option for other scenarios in a future analysis.

7 Select one of the scenarios (e.g. "X200"), and click **Show** to display the associated results on the worksheet

8 Select **Close**, to exit the **Scenario Manager** and return to the worksheet

Don't forget

You can click **Edit** to make changes or corrections to a scenario, or click **Delete** if you no longer want the selected scenario.

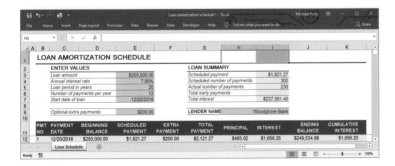

The results from the scenario that was last shown will be displayed in the worksheet. If no scenario was left selected in the **Scenario Manager**, the original worksheet values will be shown.

Summary Reports

To create a scenario summary report, showing all the possible outcomes on one worksheet:

1 On the **Data** tab, in the **Forecast** group, click **What-If Analysis**, click **Scenario Manager**, and then click **Summary...**

2 Choose report type **Scenario summary**

3 Enter the references for the cells that you want to track (cells with values modified by the changes in scenario values), in this case **I5** (actual number of payments) and **I7** (total interest)

4 The outcomes for each of the scenarios are calculated, and the results placed on the "Scenario Summary" worksheet

It isn't essential to select result cells to generate a scenario summary report, though you would normally want to include values that reflect outcomes.

Scenario Summary

	Current Values:	X000	X050	X100	X150	X200	X250	X300	X350
Changing Cells:									
LoanAmount	$250,000.00	$250,000.00	$250,000.00	$250,000.00	$250,000.00	$250,000.00	$250,000.00	$250,000.00	$250,000.00
LoanPeriod	25	25	25	25	25	25	25	25	25
ExtraPayments	$2,500.00	$0.00	$50.00	$100.00	$150.00	$200.00	$250.00	$300.00	$350.00
Result Cells:									
$I$5	72	300	278	260	244	230	219	208	199
$I$7	$64,283.22	$326,380.18	$297,454.90	$273,913.10	$254,270.11	$237,561.40	$223,132.73	$210,518.63	$199,374.51

Notes: Current Values column represents values of changing cells at time Scenario Summary Report was created. Changing cells for each scenario are highlighted in gray.

In the Scenario Summary, the **Changing Cells** section displays the values for each scenario of the cells that were selected on creation of the scenario. The **Result Cells** section shows the cell **Payments** and **Total_Interest**, specified when the summary report was created. The Current Values column shows the original values, before the scenarios were defined.

The results can also be presented as a **Scenario PivotTable** report:

1 Open the **Scenario Manager**, click **Summary**, choose **Scenario PivotTable report**, and enter the references for the result cells

2 The results are shown in a table on a separate worksheet

You must switch back to the **Loan Amortization Schedule** worksheet before opening the **Scenario Manager**.

To generate a **Scenario PivotTable report**, it is always necessary to specify the relevant result cells you desire.

3 Select the **PivotTable Tools, Analyze** tab and click **PivotChart** in the **Tools** group

4 Choose the type of chart – **Line** chart, for example – and then click **OK**

5 Make appropriate changes to the chart definition to suit the ranges of data displayed

You can adjust the **Axis Options** to display a **Secondary Vertical Value Axis** as shown here. As with any chart, you can select **Design, Move Chart**, and place the **PivotChart** on a separate worksheet.

165

Goal Seek

If you know the result that you want from an analysis, but not the input values the worksheet needs to get that result, you can use the **Goal Seek** feature. For example, you can use **Goal Seek** in the "Loan Amortization" worksheet, to determine the extra payment required to keep total interest below $150,000:

 Select **Data**, then **What-If Analysis** from the **Forecast** group, and then **Goal Seek...**

Hot tip

Start off with the original data scenario, and the extra payment value will be incremented, until the target interest level has been achieved.

Don't forget

The **By changing cell** must be referred to by the formula in the **Set cell**, where the changes should be reflected.

2 For **Set cell**, enter the reference for the cell with the target value (cell **I7**, for "Total interest")

3 In the box for the **To value**, type the result you want (i.e. 150000)

4 In the box for **By changing cell**, enter the reference for the cell that contains the value you want to adjust (**E9**, for "Optional extra payments")

Beware

The references for the **Set cell**, and for the **By changing cell**, must be to single cells only.

5 The value in **I7** is rapidly varied, and the worksheet continually recalculated, until the target value of interest is reached

6 Click **OK** to show the worksheet, with the solution in **E9**

 Save the results as another scenario, for later reference

Optimization

Goal Seek allows you to solve problems where you want to find the value of a single input, to generate the desired result. It is of no help when you need to find the best values for several inputs. For this you require an optimizer, a software tool that helps you find the best way to allocate resources. These could be raw materials, machine time, people time, money, or anything that is in limited supply. The best or optimal solution will perhaps be the one that maximizes profit, or minimizes cost, or meets some other requirement. All kinds of situations can be tackled in this way, including allocating finance, scheduling production, blending raw materials, routing goods, and loading transportation.

Excel includes an add-in optimizer, called **Solver**. You may need to install this (see page 103) if it doesn't appear on your system. To illustrate **Solver**, we'll examine a product mix problem.

Sample Solver Problem

Imagine that your hobby is textiles, and that you produce craft goods (ponchos, scarves, and gloves). There's a craft fair coming up, and you plan to use your existing inventory of materials (warp, weft, and braid) and your available time (for the loom, and to finish goods). You want to know the mix of products that will maximize profits, given the inventory and time available. These include 800 hanks of warp, 600 hanks of weft, 50 lengths of braid, 300 hours of loom time, and 200 hours of finishing time.

To produce a poncho, you will need 8 units of warp, 7 of weft, 1 of braid, 6 for loom, and 2 for finish. For a scarf, the values are 3 warp, 2 weft, 0 braid, 1 loom, and 1 finish. For a pair of gloves, they are 1 warp, 0 weft, 0 braid, 0 loom, and 4 finish.

You make the assumption that your profit is $25 per poncho, $10 per scarf, and $8 per pair of gloves.

You remember that you need four of each item as samples, to show the visitors to the fair. Also, you recall that usually, half the scarves are sold in sets with gloves.

Relationships between the objective, constraints, and decision variables are analyzed to decide the best solution, to satisfy the requirements.

The problem description must be in sufficient detail, to establish the relationships and identify the constraints.

Project Worksheet

The craft fair optimization information (see page 167) can be expressed in the following worksheet, with the underlying formulas also displayed:

The worksheet captures the information about resources available, and the amounts needed for any specified level of production.

First worksheet (values):

		Resources		Projects			Production			
		Available	Used	Poncho	Scarf	Gloves		Poncho	Scarf	Gloves
	Warp	800	310	8	3	1	Net value per item	25	10	8
	Weft	600	250	7	2	0				
	Braiding	50	30	1	0	0	Quantity created	30	20	10
	Loom	300	200	6	1	0				
	Finish	200	120	2	1	4	Total income			
							1030			

Second worksheet (formulas):

		Resources		Projects			Production			
		Available	Used	Poncho	Scarf	Gloves		Poncho	Scarf	Gloves
	Warp	800	=SUMPRODUCT(F4:H4,$K$6:$M$6)	8	3	1	Net value per item	25	10	8
	Weft	600	=SUMPRODUCT(F5:H5,$K$6:$M$6)	7	2	0				
	Braiding	50	=SUMPRODUCT(F6:H6,$K$6:$M$6)	1	0	0	Quantity created	30	20	10
	Loom	300	=SUMPRODUCT(F7:H7,$K$6:$M$6)	6	1	0				
	Finish	200	=SUMPRODUCT(F8:H8,$K$6:$M$6)	2	1	4	Total income			
							=SUMPRODUCT(K4:M4,K6:M6)			

Some constraints are specified in the problem description, while others may be implicit – e.g. the requirement for integer (and positive) values of production.

Sample values for the production quantities have been inserted, just to check that the worksheet operates as expected. Excel **Solver** will be used to compute the optimum quantities. These are limitations or constraints that must be taken into account:

1. You cannot exceed the available resources

2. There must be at least 4 of each product (samples for the craft show)

3. There must be whole numbers of products (integers)

4. There must be a pair of gloves each, for at least half the scarves (so that sets can be offered for sale)

Solver

To calculate the optimum solution for the craft fair problem:

1 Click the cell J9, which contains the target value "Total Income", then select the **Data** tab, and click **Solver** in the **Analyze** group

2 Check the **Max** option. Then, click the **By Changing Variable Cells** box, and use the collapse/expand buttons to select the product quantities cells (K6:M6)

Solver will use the currently selected cell as the target, unless you replace this reference with another cell.

3 Click the **Add** button, and select cells to specify that resources used must be less than or equal to those available

Click **Add**, to define the next constraint, or click **OK** to return to the **Solver Parameters** dialog box.

4 Click **Add**, select the cells that indicate the quantities created, and specify these are greater than or equal to 4

5 Add the constraint that the quantities created must be integers

...cont'd

6 Specify that the quantity of gloves must be at least half that of scarves, then click **OK**

Add Constraint				
Cell Reference:			Constraint:	
$M$6	⬆	>=	=$L$6/2	⬆

OK   Add   Cancel

Solver Parameters

Set Objective: $J$9

To: ● Max ○ Min ○ Value Of: 0

By Changing Variable Cells:
$K$6:$M$6

Subject to the Constraints:
$D$4:$D$8 <= $C$4:$C$8
$K$6:$M$6 = integer
$K$6:$M$6 >= 4
$M$6 >= $L$6/2

Add Change Delete Reset All Load/Save

☑ Make Unconstrained Variables Non-Negative

Select a Solving Method: GRG Nonlinear   Options

Help   Solve   Close

Hot tip

Click the box to make all unconstrained variables non-negative.

7 Click **Solve**, and the results are calculated and displayed

8 If **Solver** finds a solution, click **Keep Solver Solution**, clear **Return to Solver Parameters Dialog**, select a report if desired, then click **OK**, to return to the workbook

Solver Results

Solver found a solution. All Constraints and optimality conditions are satisfied.

Reports: Answer

● Keep Solver Solution
○ Restore Original Values

☐ Return to Solver Parameters Dialog   ☑ Outline Reports

OK   Cancel   Save Scenario...

Solver found a solution. All Constraints and optimality conditions are satisfied.

Don't forget

The **Answer Report** worksheet added each time you run **Solver** will show the detailed results, and the constraints that have been applied. Click **Save Scenario** to keep a record of the settings.

Save Scenario

Scenario Name: Craft Fair Optimum

OK   Cancel

WeavingProjects.xlsx - Excel   Michael Price

File Home Insert Page Layout Formulas Data Review View Developer Help

J9   =SUMPRODUCT(K4:M4,K6:M6)

Wool'n'Weave Project Plan

		Resources			Projects				Production		
		Available	Used	Poncho	Scarf	Gloves			Poncho	Scarf	Gloves
Warp		800	479	8	3	1	Net value per item		25	10	8
Weft		600	380	7	2	0					
Braiding		50	44	1	0	0	Quantity created		44	36	19
Loom		300	300	6	1	0					
Finish		200	200	2	1	4	Total income				
								1612			

Answer Report 1 Sheet1

Ready   100%

11 Links and Connections

Excel lets you make external references to other workbooks, or to web pages that contain data needed for your active worksheet. Your worksheet is updated automatically, if the source data changes. You can also share your data as an Office document, or as a PDF.

172 Link to Workbooks

174 Create External References

176 Styles of Reference

177 Source Workbook Changes

178 Apply the Updates

179 Turn Off the Prompt

180 Save Workbook Online

182 Using the Excel Online App

184 Excel in Word

186 Publish as PDF (or XPS)

Workbook links are very useful when you need to combine information from several workbooks that may be created in different locations, or on different systems.

Don't forget

This shows the sales by quarter, for one region, with the first two quarters entered. The calculations for margin (profit/sales) for the remaining quarters show zero divide errors, since the associated sales values are zero.

Link to Workbooks

Sometimes, you may want to refer to the data in one workbook, from another separate workbook. You may, for example, want to provide an alternative view of the data in a worksheet, or to merge data from individual workbooks, to create a summary workbook. You can refer to the contents of cells in another workbook by creating external references (also known as links).

References may be to a cell or to a range, though it is usually better to refer to a defined name in the other workbook.

To establish defined names in a source workbook:

1 Open a source workbook – **North.xlsx**, for example

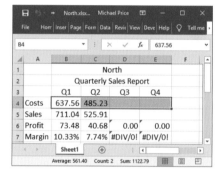

2 Select a range of cells – B4:E4 (the costs), for example

3 Select the **Formulas** tab, then click **Define Name**, from the **Defined Names** group

4 Specify the name (or accept the suggested name, based on the adjacent label "Costs"), then click **OK**

5 Repeat the **Define Name** process for "Sales" (cells B5:E5)

6 Repeat a final time, to define a name for the "Profit" values (cells B6:E6)

7 Select the **Formulas** tab and click **Name Manager**, in the **Defined Names** group, to see all the name definitions

Don't forget

The benefit of links is that when source workbooks change, you won't have to make changes manually to the destination workbooks that refer to those sources.

8 Save and close the workbook to record the names

9 Repeat this for each of the other source workbooks ("South", "East", and "West") in turn, defining range names "Costs", "Sales", and "Profit"

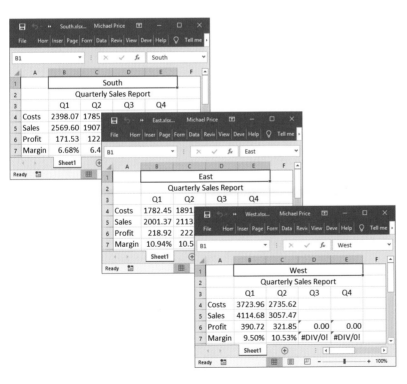

Hot tip

The names will have the same cell references for the associated ranges as those shown for the North workbook.

10 Save and close each workbook, to record the names

Create External References

  Open the source workbooks that contain the cells you want to refer to (e.g. "North", "South", "East", "West")

Open the workbook that will contain the external references (in the example, it is called **Overall.xlsx**)

Hot tip

You can incorporate the external reference into a function or formula, as you might with any cell reference.

Select the cell in which you want to create the first of the external references (e.g. B4) and type (for example) **=sum(**

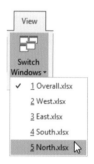

Select the **View** tab and, in the **Windows** group, click **Switch Windows**, then click the source workbook to make it active (if necessary, select the worksheet with the cells that you want to link to)

Don't forget

When you paste **Costs** into the **Overall** worksheet it is the total costs from the **North** worksheet **Costs** row.

Press **F3**, and select the defined name for the range of cells – e.g. "Costs"; click **OK**, and then press **Enter**

6 Similarly, enter a formula in B5 to sum "Sales", and enter a formula in B6 to sum "Profit"

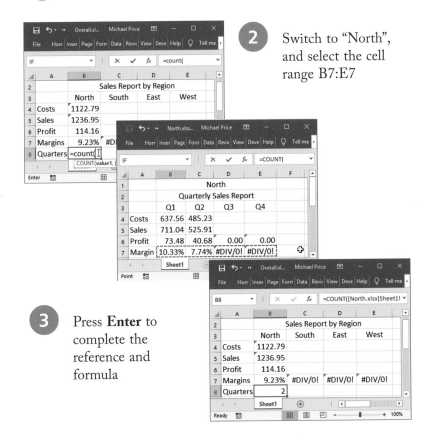

Hot tip

You can copy the formula for **Costs**, and then change the defined name to **Sales** or **Profit**.

You could refer to source workbook cells directly:

1 Click in cell B8, and type **=count(**

2 Switch to "North", and select the cell range B7:E7

Don't forget

This function counts the number of cells containing numbers (thus ignoring the incomplete quarters, where the **Margin** shows **#DIV/0!** – Divide by Zero).

3 Press **Enter** to complete the reference and formula

Styles of Reference

While the source workbooks are open, the links to defined names take the form:

North.xlsx!Costs

Where you refer to cells directly, the links take the form:

[North.xlsx]Sheet1!$B$7:$E$7

Note that the cell references could be relative or mixed, as well as absolute, as shown.

Close the source workbook, and you'll find that the external references are immediately expanded, to include a fully qualified link to the source workbook file:

Don't forget

Quotation marks will be applied to the workbook name, if it contains any spaces; for example: **'The North.xlsx'!Costs**.

	A	B	C	D	E	F	G
2			Sales Report by Region				
3		North	South	East	West		
4	Costs	1122.79	4183.39	3673.80	6459.58		
5	Sales	1236.95	4477.43	4115.15	7172.15		
6	Profit	114.16	294.04	441.35	712.57		
7	Margins	9.23%	6.57%	10.73%	9.94%		
8	Quarters	2	2	2	2		

E4 =SUM('C:\Users\mapri\Documents\West.xlsx'!Costs)

Links with direct cell references also show the fully qualified link, with file path and name:

Hot tip

The references for **South**, **East**, and **West** have been incorporated. You can do this via a selection, as with **North**, or you can just copy the formulas for **North**, and change the name appropriately.

Find and Replace

Find | Replace

Find what: North
Replace with: South

Options >>

Replace All | Replace | Close

	A	B	C	D	E	F	G	H
2			Sales Report by Region					
3		North	South	East	West			
4	Costs	1122.79	4183.39	3673.80	6459.58			
5	Sales	1236.95	4477.43	4115.15	7172.15			
6	Profit	114.16	294.04	441.35	712.57			
7	Margins	9.23%	6.57%	10.73%	9.94%			
8	Quarters	2	2	2	2			

E8 =COUNT('C:\Users\mapri\Documents\[West.xlsx]Sheet1'!$B$7:$E$7)

In each case, the path and file name will be enclosed in quotation marks, whether there are spaces included or not.

Source Workbook Changes

Assume that you receive new versions of the source workbooks (with the next quarter's data). You can control how and when these changes affect the destination workbook:

1 Open the destination workbook

2 By default, you'll receive a warning message saying there are external links, and offering an option to apply updates

> **Microsoft Excel** ✕
>
> ⚠ This workbook contains links to one or more external sources that could be unsafe.
>
> If you trust the links, update them to get the latest data. Otherwise, you can keep working with the data you have.
>
> [Update]   [Don't Update]   [Help]

3 Select **Don't Update**, and the workbook opens, unchanged

	A	B	C	D	E	F
1				Overall		
2			Sales Report by Region			
3			North	South	East	West
4	Costs	1122.79	4183.39	3673.80	6459.58	
5	Sales	1236.95	4477.43	4115.15	7172.15	
6	Profit	114.16	294.04	441.35	712.57	
7	Margins	9.23%	6.57%	10.73%	9.94%	
8	Quarters	2	2	2	2	

B1   *fx*   Overall

4 Select **File**, **Options**, then

Account
Feedback
Options

5 Click **Advanced** and review the **General** settings; i.e. "Ask to update automatic links"

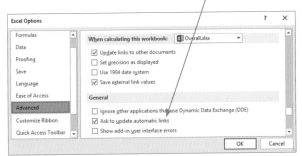

> **Excel Options**   ? ✕
>
> Formulas
> Data
> Proofing
> Save
> Language
> Ease of Access
> **Advanced**
> Customize Ribbon
> Quick Access Toolbar
>
> When calculating this workbook: [X] Overall.xlsx
> ☑ Update links to other documents
> ☐ Set precision as displayed
> ☐ Use 1904 date system
> ☑ Save external link values
>
> **General**
> ☐ Ignore other applications that use Dynamic Data Exchange (DDE)
> ☑ Ask to update automatic links
> ☐ Show add-in user interface errors
>
> [OK]   [Cancel]

Don't forget

Leave source workbooks closed. When source and destination workbooks are open at the same time on the same computer, links will be updated automatically.

Hot tip

Select **Update** and the source workbooks will be accessed, and any changes will be applied when the destination workbook opens.

Beware

Do not use this option to turn off the prompt, or you will not be aware when workbooks get updated. Use the workbook-specific option (see page 179) instead.

Apply the Updates

Select the **Data** tab, then, in the **Connections** group, choose the command **Edit Links**

Select the links to refresh, and click **Update Values**

You can choose to only update selected entries, and you can use the **Check Status** button to see which entries still need to be applied.

Do not apply updates where you are unsure of the origin of the changes, or if you want to retain current values.

Data changes are applied, and the worksheet status is updated from "Unknown" to "OK"

The updated information is added to the destination workbook, which now displays the data for three quarters

To see trends in **Costs**, select cell F4, click **Insert**, pick a **Sparklines** type and select data range (B4:E4).

Copy F4 to F5:F7 to see trends in **Sales**, **Profit**, and **Margins**.

Turn Off the Prompt

If you are confident with the integrity of the external links, you can turn off the update prompt for a specific workbook. To do this:

 Open the workbook and select **Edit Links** from the **Connections** group on the **Data** tab

 Click the **Startup Prompt...** button and choose **Don't display the alert and update links**, then click **OK**

③ Whenever you open that workbook in future, Excel will automatically check for updates and apply the latest values from the source workbooks

④ The Overall workbook now displays data for four quarters

Don't forget

If you choose **Don't display the alert and don't update automatic links**, users of the workbook won't be aware when the data in the workbook becomes out of date.

Hot tip

This shows the effect when you open the destination workbook after updates have been applied to the source workbooks.

Save Workbook Online

You can store workbooks and other documents online, and access them via Office Online apps, or share them with other users.
To copy a workbook to OneDrive from within Excel:

 Open a workbook, click the **File** tab, and select **Save As**

Hot tip

You can also access your OneDrive from Office Online in **office. microsoft.com** (see page 20) or from the OneDrive feature in Windows 10.

Hot tip

Choose **Share** on the Excel 2019 Ribbon to share your spreadsheet quickly with others on SharePoint or OneDrive.

Don't forget

You could save the workbook in your private documents folder or in your public folder, but for controlled access, click **New** and create a separate OneDrive folder.

2 Select the OneDrive for the current user and click **Browse** to explore the OneDrive contents

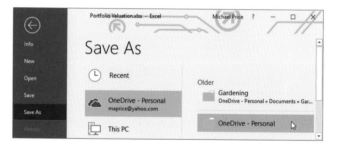

3 Select the OneDrive folder where you'll put the workbook ("Project", for example), and click **Open**

4 Amend the workbook name if required, and click **Save**

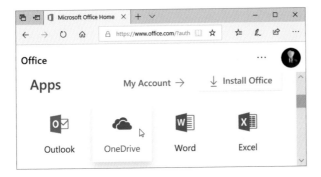

With the workbook on your OneDrive, you can now access it via your browser, even on computers that do not have a copy of the Excel 2019 application installed.

1 Go online to **office.com** and sign in using the email address that is associated with your Microsoft Account

2 Scroll down to the Apps, and select the icon to access your OneDrive

Using the Excel Online App

 1 Having opened your OneDrive, click the folder that contains the workbook you want to view

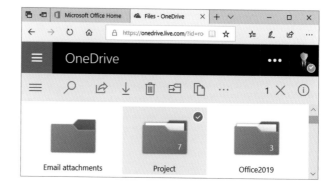

You can have up to 5GB of free storage on your OneDrive. You can purchase additional storage for an annual fee *(correct at the time of printing)*.

 2 When the folder opens, right-click the workbook to display the options that are available

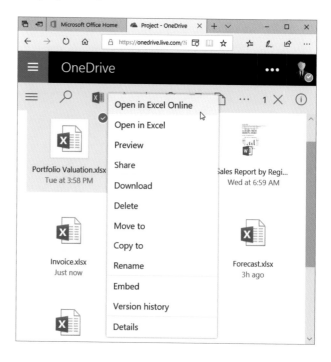

You can right-click the file or folder in your OneDrive and select Share, to send a link by email to allow other users to access the workbook via their browsers or via Excel 2019 if installed.

 3 Select the entry to **Open in Excel Online**

...cont'd

Since not all features of Excel 2019 are supported in the Excel Online app, you are advised to edit a copy of the file.

When you try to open a workbook in Excel Online, you'll be warned if it is already open and you won't be allowed to edit it in Excel Online.

4 Select **Edit a Copy**, provide a name (or accept the suggested name) and click **Save**

5 The workbook opens in your browser ready to edit

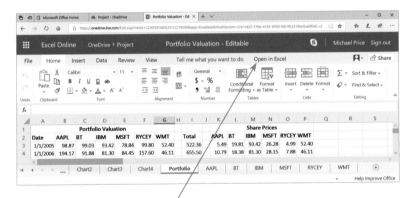

6 Click **Open in Excel** to switch to the full Excel 2019

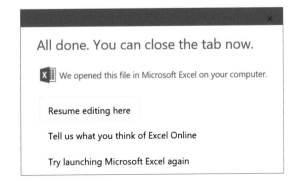

You need a supported version of Microsoft Excel on your computer to open the workbook in Excel. If necessary, you can install a trial copy of Office 2019.

Excel in Word

Hot tip

To share data with others who don't have access to Excel or the Office Online apps, you can present the information in a Microsoft Office Word document (as illustrated here), or in a PowerPoint presentation.

Don't forget

You can paste the data as a table, retaining the original formatting, or using styles from the Word document, as shown. Alternatively, paste the data as a picture or tab-separated text. There are also options to maintain a link with the original worksheet.

To add data from an Excel worksheet to a Word document:

  In Excel, select the worksheet data, and press **Ctrl + C** (or select **Home** and click **Copy**, from the **Clipboard** group)

	North	South	East	West
Costs	2676.06	9516.33	6802.92	16172.34
Sales	2946.58	10477.55	7557.57	17822.25
Profit	270.52	961.22	754.65	1649.91
Margins	9.18%	9.17%	9.99%	9.26%
Quarters	4	4	4	4

2 Click in the Word document, and press **Ctrl + V** (or select **Home** and click **Paste**, from the **Clipboard** group)

Sales Report by Region

Please find attached the sales report by region, with the percent margins. West remains the leading region by sales, but East now boasts the highest margin.

The detailed figures for costs, sales and profit are as follows:

The results are also available in chart form:

  3 Click **Paste Options**, and select the type of paste you want

The detailed figures for costs, sales and profit are as follows:

	North	South	East	West
Costs	2676.06	9516.33	6802.92	16172.34
Sales	2946.58	10477.55	7557.57	17822.25
Profit	270.52	961.22	754.65	1649.91
Margins	9.18%	9.17%	9.99%	9.26%

The results are also available in chart form:

  4 The data from the workbook is inserted in the document

To copy an Excel chart to your Word document:

1 In Excel, select the chart on the worksheet or chart sheet, and press **Ctrl** + **C** (or select **Home**, **Copy**)

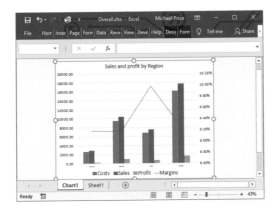

2 In the Word document, click where you want the chart, and press **Ctrl** + **V** (or select **Home**, **Paste**)

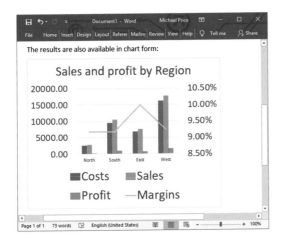

3 Click **Paste Options**, and select the type you want

Publish as PDF (or XPS)

To send data to others who do not have Excel or Word, you can publish the workbook in Adobe Acrobat PDF format, or XPS format. The recipient only need have any suitable viewing app, such as Acrobat Reader, Microsoft Reader, or XPS Viewer. To do this:

Hot tip

Microsoft Reader in Windows 10 can read both PDF and XPS files. XPS Viewer can be used in previous versions.

1 Open the workbook in Excel, click the **File** tab, and then click **Save As**

2 Set the **Save as type** drop-down box to PDF (or to XPS)

Don't forget

You can publish the entire workbook, the active worksheet or selected ranges of cells as PDF or XPS documents.

3 Click the **Options...** button, to set the scope – e.g. **Active sheet(s)** or **Entire workbook** – and click **OK**

4 Check **Open file after publishing**, then click **Save** to create and display the PDF (or XPS) file

Hot tip

If you save your workbooks as PDF (or XPS) files, you can be sure that the files you share retain exactly the data and format you intended.

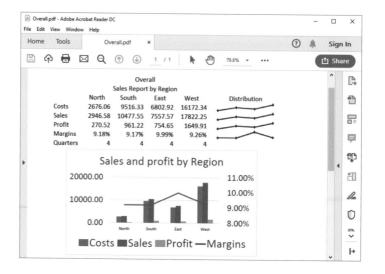

Overall
Sales Report by Region

	North	South	East	West
Costs	2676.06	9516.33	6802.92	16172.34
Sales	2946.58	10477.55	7557.57	17822.25
Profit	270.52	961.22	754.65	1649.91
Margins	9.18%	9.17%	9.99%	9.26%
Quarters	4	4	4	4

Index

Symbols

2-D charts	125-126, 130, 135
3-D charts	132-133, 135
32-bit or 64-bit systems	12
### errors	69

A

Absolute reference	10, 62
Adobe Acrobat Reader	186
Advanced options	106
Age	95
Alignment	
Merge & Center	30
Numbers	24
Text	24, 30, 60
Alignment group	22
Analysis	
Group	103
ToolPak	103
What-If	162-163
Argument.	See Function: Arguments
Arithmetic operators	64
Array	10, 23
Arrow keys	44
Audit formula	106
Trace dependent	107
Trace precedent	106-107
AutoComplete	67
AutoFit column	27
AutoRecover	112
AutoSave	112
AutoSum	27, 29, 68, 117
AVERAGE function	101

B

BackStage	11, 16
Back up workbook	111
Bar chart	124
Base year	94
Basic Programming.	See Visual Basic

C

Calculation sequence	65
Calendar effects	94
Cell reference	23
Cells group	22
Chart	
Create	124-125
Data table	128
In Word	185
Layout	16, 125, 127
Legend	128
Move	125
Print	138
Rotation	132
Tools	125, 131-133
Types	126, 129-133, 135-137
Charts group	125
CHOOSE function	91
Clipboard	22, 81, 184-185
Collapse Dialog button	66, 92
Collapse Ribbon	118
Column	23
AutoFit	27
Hide	55
Insert	26
Select	27
Table	72-73
Width	27, 55
Column chart	133
Comma delimited file	38
Command tabs	18, 22
Comments	70
Concatenate	95
Control Panel	59
CONVERT function	102
Copy	34, 81, 184-185
Copy cells	28
Copy file	111
COUNT function	101
Count unique	77
CSV file	38, 40

D

Data arrays	23
Data import	42-43

Data sort	48
Data tab	
Edit links	178-179
Get text	80
New functions	103
Remove duplicates	52
Scenario Manager	162-165
Solver	169-170
Sort	82
What-if analysis	162-164
Date and time format	59, 94
Date & Time functions	94-95
Delete	
Columns	29
Rows	29
Table column	74
Table row	74
Design tab	73
Developer tab	141
Add	141
Macros	145, 150-154
Record macro	142-143
Use relative references	142
Visual Basic	150
Dialog box	22
Dialog button	66
Document recovery	112
Document Theme	11
Duplicate entries	52

E

Editing group	22, 48
Edit links	178-179
End key	47
Engineering functions	102
Error checking	109-110
Evaluate formula	104
Excel	
Add-ins	103, 167
Help	35
In PowerPoint	184
In Word	184-185
Resources	160
Solver	168-169
Versions	10, 72
Excel List	72
Excel Online app.	See Office Online apps
Excel program shortcut	114
Excel Table	72-73
Excel window	22-23

Expand Dialog button	66, 92
External reference	172, 174-176

F

Field settings	85
File format	11, 37-38, 40
File tab	11, 16, 22, 32, 119
BackStage	11, 16
Close	143
New	156
Open	42, 111
Options	103, 106, 109, 112, 140-141
Print	83, 121, 138
Save	25
Save As	37-38, 43, 186
Fill Handle	28
Filter	48, 50
Filter box	73, 82
Financial functions	92-93
Find	49
Find duplicates	52
Font group	22
Format	
Date and time	59, 94
General	31, 43, 60
Numbers	31, 58-59
Text	30, 60
Formula	9, 26
Auditing	104, 106-107
Errors	69, 109-110
Evaluate	104
Protect	108
Show	108
Formula Bar	22
Formulas tab	
New functions	103
Freeze headers	54
Function	
Arguments	66, 92
AutoComplete	67
Insert	66, 88
Function Library	68, 88
Functions	
Date & Time	94-95
Engineering	102
Financial	92-93
Lookup & Reference	90-91
Math & Trig	98-99
Most Recently Used	88
Statistical	101
Text	96-97

G

General format	31, 43, 58, 60
Get Office	13
Goal Seek	166-167
Green flash	69
Group	
Alignment	22
Cells	22
Clipboard	22
Editing	22
Font	22
Formula Auditing	109
Function Library	68
Macros	141
Number	22
Styles	22
Tables	73

H

Hash signs	69
Help	35, 69
Contextual	36
Hide columns and rows	55
Home key	47
Home tab	22
AutoSum	29, 68
Cell Styles	86
Copy	81
Delete	74
Find & Select	49
Font	30
Format	27, 55-56, 58, 108
Insert	26, 34, 79
Merge & Center	30
Paste	101
Sort & Filter	48, 50, 82
Horizontal lookup	90

I

Import data	40-43, 80
Insert	
Column	26, 34
Function	88
Row	26, 34, 80-81
Table column	79
Table row	80
Insert tab	116
Charts	125, 130
PivotTable	84-85
Table	72-73
Internet resources	150, 160-161
Interval	95

J

Join	95

K

Keyboard shortcuts	25, 36, 38, 40, 47, 49, 62, 83, 108, 115, 121
Keystroke navigation	47
Key Tips	115-118, 121

L

Label	
Column	25
Row	25
Layout	
Chart	16, 125, 127
Page	33, 108
Ledger sheet	8
Line chart	135
Lookup function	90
Lookup table	134
Lotus 123	8, 10

M

Macros	140
Add to toolbar	152-153
Cell references	143, 146

Create	141, 150-151
Debug	154
Edit	145, 148
Record	142-143
Run	144, 149, 151, 152
Save	142-143
Security	140, 143
View	145
Math & Trig functions	98-99
MAX function	101
Maximize Ribbon	22
Measurement systems	102
MEDIAN function	101
Memory requirements	12
Merge & Center text	30
Microsoft Office 2019	11, 13
MIN function	101
Mini Toolbar	120
Mixed reference	62
MODE function	101
Mouse	
Control Panel	46
Scroll with	46
Move cells	34
Move chart	125

N

Name	
Box	22
Define	63, 172
Manager	63, 73, 157, 173
Reference	63
Nested functions	69
Number	
Alignment	24
Format	31, 58-59
Group	22
Negative	31, 58, 72, 92
Roman	102
Number systems	102

O

Office	
Compatibility	12
File formats	12
Office 365	11, 13
Office 2019	11
Requirements	12
Ribbon	16-17, 183
Versions	10
Windows 10	12, 14-15
Office Online apps	11, 20, 180, 184
Excel Online app	20, 182-183
OneDrive	56, 111, 180, 182
Online templates	158-159
OpenXML	11
Operating system	
Requirements	12
Operator precedence	65
Operators	64
Optimizer	167

P

Page keys	47
Page Layout	33, 108
Page Setup	122
Parentheses	65
Paste	34, 81, 184-185
Paste Values	101
PDF	186
Personal Macro Workbook	142-145, 149
Perspective	
2-D	130
3-D	132-133
Pie chart	130-132
Pin to Start menu	114
Pin to taskbar	114
PivotChart	165
PivotTable	84-85, 165
PMT function	92
PowerPoint	10, 184
Print	
Charts	138
Preview	32
Table	83
Worksheet	32-33, 121-122
Processor requirements	12
PRODUCT function	98
Program shortcut	114
Protect	
Formula	108
Worksheet	56, 73, 108

Q

Quick Access Toolbar   22, 119, 153
Quick Styles   75

R

Random numbers   100
Range   86
Recalculate   110
Recalculation   8, 10
Red flash   70
Reference
   Absolute   10, 62-63
   Cell   23
   External   172, 174-177
   Mixed   62
   Name   63, 172
   Relative   10, 61
   Structured   78
Relative reference   10
Remove duplicates   52
Rename sheet   29
Review tab   53, 70
Ribbon   11, 16-17, 22
   Collapse   118
   Display   118
   Key Tips   115-118
   Tabs   18
Roman numerals   102
ROUND function   99
Row   23
Row height   55

S

Save workbook   25, 37-38
Scenario
   Delete   163
   Edit   163
   PivotTable   165
   Summary report   164-165
Scenario Manager   162-165
Scroll   22-23, 44-46
Scroll bar   22-23, 45
Scroll Lock   44

Secondary axis   137
Shared Office features   11, 16
Share price data   124, 134, 146-149
Sheet.   See Worksheet
Show formula   61, 108, 157
Show margins   122
Solutions group   103
Solver Add-in   103, 167-170
Sort rows   48, 82
Sparklines   178
Special format   58
Spell check   53
Split view   45
Spreadsheet.   See Worksheet
Spreadsheet concept   8-9
Stacked column chart   125
Startup switches   113
Statistical functions   101
Status bar   22
Stock chart   136
Stock symbols   128
Structured Reference   78
Sum.   See AutoSum
System requirements   12

T

Tab delimited file   38, 41
Tab key   47
Table
   Calculated column   79
   Column   72-73
      Delete   74
      Insert   79
   Create   72-73, 146-147
   Name   73, 78
   Print   83
   Row   72
      Delete   74
      Insert   74, 80-81
   Style   75
   Summarize   84-85
   Tools   73, 86
   Totals   76
Tables group   73
Tag word   25
Tell Me box   35
Templates   156-159
Text
   Alignment   24, 30
   Format   30, 60

Orientation	60
Wrap	60
Text functions	96-97
Title bar	22
Toolbar	
Customize	152-153
Mini	120
Quick Access	119
Tooltips	36
Trace	
Dependent	107
Empty cell	110
Error	110
Precedent	106-107
Truncated entries	27

Windows 10	12, 14-15
Word	10, 184
Word Count	97
Workbook	22
Build	26-27
Create	24
Link	172-173, 176, 184-185
Update	177
Protect	56, 177
Save	25
Worksheet	22
Navigate	44-45
Print	32-33
Tabs	22
Wrap Text	60

U

Unfreeze	54
Update link	177-179
Update prompt	179
Username	70

V

VBA.	*See* Visual Basic
Vertical lookup	79, 90
View macros	141, 145, 152
Views	22
View tab	
Freeze panes	54
Hide/Unhide	145
Macros	141, 154
Switch windows	174
VisiCalc	8, 10
Visual Basic	140, 150
Visual Basic Editor	143, 148

W

What-If	
Analysis	162
Goal Seek	166

X

XY view	132

Y

Yahoo! Finance	134, 137
Yahoo! share data	134, 146-149

Z

Zoom	32
Zoom slider	22